BRIDGE
at your fingertips

AMALYA KEARSE

A HART BOOK

A & W VISUAL LIBRARY
NEW YORK

PUBLISHED BY
A & W PUBLISHERS, INC.
95 MADISON AVENUE
NEW YORK, NEW YORK 10016

LIBRARY OF CONGRESS CATALOG CARD NO. 79-88566

ISBN: 0-89104-159-1

PRINTED IN THE UNITED STATES OF AMERICA

CONTENTS

Basics

Notrump Openings & Sequences

One-Level Suit Openings and Sequences

Openings of 2 of a Suit

Pre-Emptive Opening Bids

Opening above the Game Level

Opening with a Part-Score

Slam Bidding

Notrump Overcalls

Suit Overcalls

Takeout Doubles

Penalty Doubles

Cue-Bids in Opponent's Suits

Re-Opening the Bidding — "Balancing"

Alternative Systems and Conventions

Declarer Play

Defensive Play

Basics

POINT COUNT VALUES

Standard bidding is, generally speaking, based on evaluating hands by points.

HIGH CARD POINTS

Honor cards are assigned the following values:

Ace	=	4 points
King	=	3 points
Queen	=	2 points
Jack	=	1 point

Tens have no point value, but a hand rich in 10's is obviously more valuable than a hand with the same point count lacking such cards.

SHORT SUIT POINTS

In evaluating a hand for play in a suit contract, points may be assigned to certain suits that contain fewer than three cards.

Before one's partner has bid, points are added for distribution as follows:

Void = 3 points
Singleton = 2 points
Doubleton = 1 point

A player whose partner has bid should re-evaluate his hand in light of whether or not his cards are likely to help his partner's hand.

If partner bids strongly in a suit in which one holds fewer than three cards, one should not count any distributional points in that suit.

In contrast, if the player has three or more cards in his partner's suit and plans to support his partner's suit, he is entitled to make two types of upward adjustments in his distributional evaluation. He should count a King in his partner's suit as 4 points, a Queen as 3 points, and a Jack as 2 points, so long as the total he claims for that suit does not exceed 4 points.

In addition, he is entitled to count the following distributional points for his short suits:

Void = 5 points
Singleton = 3 points
Doubleton = 1 point

If his raise is made with only three card support for his partner, the player should reduce the total points counted by one.

LONG SUIT POINTS

In evaluating a hand for play in notrump ("NT"), short suit points are not counted. If the hand contains a good five- or six-card suit, however, length points may be assigned as follows:

Six-card suit = 2 points
Five-card suit = 1 point

QUICK TRICKS

In addition to high card points and distributional points, the defensive strength of a hand must frequently be considered. The calculation of defensive tricks, also called QUICK TRICKS, is based on how many of the first two tricks in a suit one is likely to win.

The following honor combinations are counted as quick tricks:

Ace   = 1
Ace and King   = 2
Ace and Queen   = 1½
King and Queen   = 1
King and another card   = ½

POINT REQUIRED FOR GAME AND SLAM

The combination of high card points and distributional points is sometimes referred to as TOTAL POINTS, or simply POINTS.

There are, in all, 40 high card points in the deck. The point count recommendations for contracts of various levels use the 40 point total as a framework—even though when distribution is counted, there are usually far more than 40 total points in the hands of the four players.

For a game contract in NT (9 tricks) or in a major suit (10 tricks)	26 points are needed.
For game in a minor suit (11 tricks)	29 points are needed.
For a small slam contract (12 tricks)	33 points are needed.
For a grand slam contract (13 tricks)	37 points are needed.

Notrump Openings & Sequences

NOTRUMP OPENINGS

All NT openings promise that the opener has a hand of well- defined strength with even distribution, and with at least three of the suits well guarded. These are the most precise of all opening bids.

STRENGTH PROMISED BY NOTRUMP OPENINGS

1 NT opening bid   Promises 16, 17, or 18 high card points.

2 NT opening bid   Promises 22, 23, or 24 high card points.

3 NT opening bid   Promises 25, 26, or 27 high card points.

4 NT opening bid   Promises 28 or 29 high card points, or a hand that will take 10 tricks.

5 NT opening bid   Does not show precise point count but guarantees that eleven tricks can be made.

6 NT opening bid   Does not show exact point count but guarantees that twelve tricks can be made.

Not all evenly distributed hands may be opened in NT. A hand worth 13-15 high card points or 19-21 high card points should be opened with a suit bid.

Opener can then *rebid* one NT to show 13 or 14 or 15 high card points, or rebid 2 NT to show 19, 20, or 21 high card points.

In all the examples throughout this book, the letter "x" is used to represent a low card whose rank is considered insignificant.

Examples:

(a)   ♠ J x x   ♡ A K x   ◇ Q x x   ♣ A J x x

Worth 15 high card points. Should be opened with 1♣, and 1 NT should be rebid.

(b)   ♠ Q J x x   ♡ A K   ◇ Q x x   ♣ A J x x

Worth 17 high card points. Should be opened with 1 NT.

(c)   ♠ A J x   ♡ A K x   ◇ Q x x   ♣ A J x x

Worth 19 high card points. Should be opened with 1♣ and the rebid should be 2 NT.

(d)   ♠ A K x x   ♡ A Q x   ◊ K Q x   ♣ A J x

Worth 23 high card points. Should be opened with 2 NT.

(e)   ♠ A K x   ♡ A x   ◊ A K Q x x   ♣ K Q x

Worth 25 high card points. Should be opened with 3 NT.

(f)   ♠ A K Q   ♡ A K Q   ◊ A K Q   ♣ Q J 10 9

Has eleven sure tricks and should be opened with 5 NT.

(g)   ♠ A K   ♡ A K Q J x x x   ◊ K Q   ♣ A K

Has 12 sure playing tricks. Should be opened with 6 NT.

DISTRIBUTIONS REQUIRED FOR NOTRUMP OPENINGS

To open the bidding in NT, a player should have no voids, no singletons, and at most one doubleton.

The appropriate distributions are therefore 4-3-3-3, 4-4-3-2, and 5-3-3-2.

The five-card suit in the last distribution may be either a minor or a major.

Occasionally, a hand with two doubletons may be opened 1 NT, if an opening bid in a suit would create serious problems for opener on his turn to rebid.

Example:

♠ K Q x   ♡ K x   ◊ Q 10 x x x x   ♣ A Q

The bidding may be opened 1 NT to forestall rebid problems. If opener had bid one diamond, he would not be able to rebid 1 NT because he has too many points. Nor could he rebid 2 NT because he has too few points. Nor could he rebid 3 ◇ because his suit is too weak.

SUIT TEXTURE REQUIRED FOR NOTRUMP OPENINGS

To open a hand with 1 NT, a player should have high cards guarding at least three of the four suits. To constitute adequate guards, or stoppers, a Queen must be accompanied by at least two cards, and a Jack must be accompanied by at least three cards.

Examples:

(a)   ♠ x x x   ♡ A K J x   ◇ x x x   ♣ A K Q

Has two unstopped suits (spades and diamonds). The opening bid should be 1♡ rather than 1 NT.

(b)   ♠ J x x   ♡ A Q x x   ◇ Q x   ♣ A K x x

Has two unstopped suits since neither Q x or J x x constitutes an adequate guard. The hand should be opened with 1♣ rather than 1 NT.

(c)   ♠ Q J x   ♡ A Q x   ◇ x x x   ♣ A K x x

Has stoppers in three suits. Should be opened 1 NT.

If the hand contains a weak doubleton, in other words, a doubleton not headed by the Ace, King, or Queen, a 1 NT opening should be avoided if there is another convenient opening and rebid.

Examples:

(d)   ♠ A Q x x   ♡ x x   ◊ A J x x   ♣ K Q J

With its weak doubleton in hearts, this hand should not be opened with 1 NT, since opener can comfortably open 1◊ and can rebid 1♠ over a 1♡ response, or bid 3♣ over a 2♣ response.

(e)   ♠ x x   ♡ A Q x   ◊ A J x x x   ♣ K Q J

With its weak doubleton spade, this hand would present a rebid problem over a 1♠ response to a 1◊ opening. The hand should be opened 1 NT despite its flaw.

To open 2 NT or higher, a player should have all four suits guarded.

Examples:

(f)   ♠ A K J   ♡ K Q J x   ◊ Q J x   ♣ K Q x

An appropriate 2 NT opening.

(g)   ♠ A K x   ♡ K Q J x   ◊ x x   ♣ A K Q x

Does not have a diamond stopper. The hand should be opened with 1♣; opener can rebid 3 NT over a 1◊ response, 4♡ over a 1♡ response, or 3♡ over a 1♠ response.

RESPONSES TO 1 NOTRUMP OPENINGS

Since the 1 NT opening promises precisely 16-18 high card points and a balanced hand, it is usually responder who takes charge of the direction of the hand. Responder determines how high to aim, and whether to try for a suit contract or a NT contract.

The rules that follow assume that neither opponent has entered the auction.

HOW HIGH RESPONDER SHOULD AIM

Responder should always bear in mind that the partnership should reach game with a combined total of 26 points, a small slam with a combined 33 points, or a grand slam with a combined 37 points.

After an opening bid in NT, responder should count his points and add them to the number of points promised by opener to ascertain whether there are enough points for game or for a slam. If he believes the final contract will be in NT, he should count high-card and long-suit points. If he envisions a final suit contract, he may rely on high-card and short-suit points.

Opposite a 1 NT opening showing 16 to 18 high card points, responder should act according to the following table:

With 0- 7 points	Sign off.
With 8- 9 points	Try for game.
With 10-14 points	Force to game.
With 15-16 points	Try for a small slam.

With 17-18 points	Force to a small slam.
With 19-20 points	Try for a grand slam.
With 21-24 points	Force to a grand slam.

ENCOURAGING AND DISCOURAGING RESPONSES TO 1 NOTRUMP OPENING

To implement his desire to reach a game or a slam, or to settle for a part-score, responder must know which responses will force opener to bid, which will invite him to bid, and which will forbid him to bid.

The only responses to a 1 NT opening that are forcing are:

2♣   The Stayman convention, asking opener if he has a four card major suit. The 2♣ response forces opener to bid, but does not guarantee another bid from responder.

3♣, 3◇,   These jumps are forcing to game and show slam in-
3♡, 3♠   terest.

4♣   The Gerber convention, asking opener how many Aces he has.

5 NT   This bid shows 19-20 points and asks opener to bid 7 NT if he has a maximum (17 or 18 points). The bid forces him to bid 6 NT without a maximum (16 points).

The only response to a 1 NT opening that immediately invites opener to bid a game is the response of 2 NT. All other invitations to game must be made by a series of bids by responder that start with 2♣, the Stayman Convention.

There are three responses to a 1 NT opening that, while not forcing, are invitational to slam. A response of 4 NT invites opener to bid 6 NT if he has a maximum (17-18 points); opener is required to pass, however, if he has only a minimum (16 points). Responses of 5♡ and 5♠ invite opener to bid a small slam in the suit with maximum strength in Aces and Kings.

Most of the responses to a 1 NT opening instruct opener not to bid again. These responses are as follows.

A response of 2♢, 2♡, or 2♠ is a sign off in that suit. It indicates that responder has less than eight points and has five or more cards in the suit he has bid. Opener is not invited to bid again.

A response of exactly game is a sign off. Thus, a jump to 3 NT, 4♡, 4♠, 5♣, or 5♢ over the 1 NT opening signifies that responder wishes to play in the game he has bid, but has no interest in trying for slam. Opener must not bid again.

A response at the six level is a sign off in the small slam and does not invite opener to bid a grand slam.

CHOOSING BETWEEN A SUIT AND NOTRUMP
FOR THE FINAL CONTRACT

In choosing between a suit and NT for the final contract, several factors are important.

If the partnership is weak in one or more suits in which the defense could take a number of tricks, NT should usually be avoided. Thus, the presence of a doubleton in responder's hand suggest that a suit contract be considered. Conversely, if responder's hand is completely balanced, so that he cannot provide any ruffing values, a suit contract should be given less consideration.

Responder must also bear in mind that a game in a minor suit normally requires a total of 29 points, as contrasted with the 26 points needed for 3 NT, 4♡, or 4♠. Thus, when responder can see that the partnership has about 25-28 points, he should steer the final game contract into NT or a major suit rather than 5♣ or 5♢.

For a suit contract, normally at least eight trumps should be held between the two hands. Inability to discover an eight-card fit suggest that the hand be played in NT.

Sometimes the partnership will possess two eight-card fits, one divided 4-4 and the other divided less evenly. Frequently the 4-4 fit will produce one trick more than a 5-3 fit, and two tricks more than a 6-2 fit. However, the 4-4 fit does not provide as much safety against a bad trump break. Thus, for a high level contract, responder should prefer to play in the 6-2 or 5-3 fit if the partnership has an abundance of high cards and may not need ruffing tricks.

Responder's choice between a suit and NT also must take into account the texture of the potential trump suit in relation to the height of the contract envisioned. A part-score contract in a suit can often be made even if all of the top trump honors are held by the defenders. For game, however, at least one of the top three trump honors is usually needed, and for slam at least two of the top three trump honors are essential. In short, if responder is seriously considering slam, he should avoid bidding weak suits.

RESPONSES TO 1 NOTRUMP
IF RESPONDER HOLDS A BALANCED HAND WITHOUT A SHORT SUIT OR WITHOUT A FOUR-CARD MAJOR

With a hand that is shaped 4-3-3-3 (e.g., ♠ K x x   ♡ A x x x ◇ Q x x   ♣ J x x), or with a balanced hand that has a doubleton but no four card major suit (e.g., ♠ K x x   ♡ Q x   ◇ A x x x   ♣ J x x x)— responder should generally be content to play the hand in NT. Responder should take action as follows:

With 0-7 high card points	Pass.
With 8-9 high card points	Raise to 2 NT. This response invites opener to bid 3 NT with a maximum.
With 10-14 high card points	Raise to 3 NT. This is a sign off and requires opener to pass.
With 15-16 high card points	Raise to 4 NT. This is not Blackwood; it invites opener to bid 6 NT with a maximum or to pass with a minimum.
With 17-18 high card points	Raise to 6 NT. This is a sign-off.
With 19-20 high card points	Raise to 5 NT. This forces opener to bid at least 6 NT and invites him to bid 7 NT with a maximum.
With 21-24 high card points	Raise to 7 NT.

RESPONSES TO 1 NOTRUMP IF RESPONDER
HOLDS A FOUR-CARD MAJOR AND A SHORT SUIT:
THE STAYMAN CONVENTION

If responder has four hearts and/or four spades and has distribution other than 4-3-3-3, he should normally prefer to play the hand in a suit contract rather than in NT if an appropriate fit can be found.

The Stayman convention is designed to locate a 4-4 major suit fit in the partnership hands after an opening bid in NT.

The operation of the convention is simple:

Responder bids 2♣ (which does not promise anything in clubs) to ask opener if he has a biddable (Q x x x or better) four card major suit.

If opener has no four-card major he rebids 2◇. The 2◇ bid does not promise diamonds, but merely denies a four card major.

If opener has four hearts, he bids 2♡. If he has four spades, he bids 2♠; if he has four hearts and four spades, he bids 2♡.

The Stayman convention is used in two principal situations. **First, it is used when responder has 8 or more high card points, at least one four-card major, and at least one doubleton.**

If responder has 8-9 points, he will invite to game—either by raising the major suit bid by opener, or by bidding 2 NT. If responder has 10 or more points, he will either bid a game, or force to game by bidding a new suit at the three level.

The second use of the Stayman convention occurs when responder has a weaker hand with two four-card majors and four or five diamonds. With such a hand, responder uses Stayman in order to escape from 1 NT.

The Stayman convention may be used even if responder has a long minor suit along with his four-card major. Since a minor suit game normally requires 29 points, responder should usually prefer to use Stayman in search of the major suit game.

When responding to a 1 NT opening with a four-card major suit and shortness in another suit, responder should take the following actions.

With 0-7 points	Responder may bid 2♣, intending to pass opener's rebid, if he has at least four cards in spades, hearts, and diamonds. Without such distribution, responder should pass unless he has a six-card suit.
With 8-9 points	Bid 2♣ intending to raise to 3♡ or 3♠ if a 4-4 major fit is found, or to rebid 2 NT if no such fit is found.
With 10-14 points	Bid 2♣ intending to raise to 4♡ or 4♠ if a 4-4 major fit is found, or to rebid 3 NT if no such fit is found.
With 15 or more points	Bid 2♣ intending to follow with a slam try by bidding a new suit or making a bid that is more than enough for game in that denomination.

Examples:

(a)   ♠ K x x x   ♡ Q x   ◊ K x x   ♣ x x x x

Responder bids 2♣, hoping to hear opener rebid 2♠. In this event, responder will raise to 3♠ to invite game. If instead, opener rebids 2◊ or 2♡, responder will rebid 2 NT, promising 8 to 9 points and indicating that his four-card major suit was spades. The 2 NT rebid by responder invites opener to bid game with a maximum. If opener has bid 2♡ with four

*hearts and four spades, he may, over responder's 2 NT, re-
bid 3♠ with a minimum and 4♠ with a maximum.*

(b)   ♠ Q J x x   ♡ K x   ◊ A x x x x   ♣ x x

*Responder bids 2♣ Stayman. If opener rebids 2♠, respond-
er will raise to 4♠. If opener rebids 2◊ or 2♡, responder
will rebid 3 NT.*

(c)   ♠ J x x x   ♡ x x x x   ◊ Q x x x   ♣ x

*Responder bids 2♣, intending to pass any rebid by opener.
He expects to fare better in a suit contract than in NT.*

(d)   ♠ K x x x   ♡ x x   ◊ 10 x x x x x   ♣ x

*Responder cannot afford to bid 2♣ Stayman, because he
would not want to pass 2♡ and has insufficient strength to
bid 2 NT over opener's rebid. He could not rebid 2♠ over
opener's rebid, for that bid would promise not only 8-9
points, but five spades as well.*

(e)   ♠ K Q x x   ♡ A x   ◊ K x x x x   ♣ x

*Responder should bid 2♣, intending to rebid 3◊ over
opener's rebid; the 3◊ rebid is forcing to game and carries
slam interest implications. It is ambiguous, however, in that
it nether confirms nor denies that responder has four cards
in the major suit bid by opener. Responder will clarify this
later—by returning to spades if opener has bid spades, or by
returning to NT if opener has bid hearts or diamonds.*

Stayman should not be used when responder's hand is completely balanced.

Examples:

(f)   ♠ Q x x   ♡ K x x   ◊ Q x x   ♣ x x x

Responder should pass 1 NT since he has no ruffing values.

(g)   ♠ Q J x x   ♡ A x x   ◊ Q J x   ♣ x x x

Responder should jump to 3 NT.

Stayman should not be used when responder has inadequate strength to take appropriate action over opener's possible responses.

Examples:

(h)   ♠ J x   ♡ A Q x x   ◊ x x x x   ♣ x x x

Responder should pass 1 NT because he does not have enough points to rebid over opener's possible 2♠ rebid.

(i)   ♠ J x x x   ♡ x x x x   ◊ x   ♣ Q x x x

Responder should pass 1 NT because he could not pass a 2◊ rebid by opener, and he does not have enough points to rebid anything.

Stayman normally should not be used when responder has a six-card major and a four-card minor, since the 6-2 fit will more often provide more tricks as the trump suit.

Example:

(j)   ♠ K J x x x x   ♡ K x x x   ◊ x x   ♣ x

Responder should jump to 4♠ rather than trying to locate a 4-4 heart fit, since having spades as trumps may provide better control of the hand and make responder's hand more useful.

RESPONSES TO 1 NOTRUMP IF RESPONDER HOLDS A FIVE-CARD OR LONGER MAJOR SUIT

If responder has a major suit that contains five or more cards, he should normally attempt to play the hand in that suit unless he has a very weak hand with only a five-card suit and no singletons.

If responder has 8-9 points and a five-card suit, he should invite game by starting with a 2♣ Stayman response. If opener does not rebid in responder's long suit, responder will bid two of his suit. This sequence promises five cards in whichever major responder bids.

If responder has a six-card suit and 7-9 points, he should jump to game in his suit. This is a sign off. Opener is not permitted to bid further.

If responder has 10-14 points, he should force to game. If he has a one-suited hand with five cards in his major suit, or has five cards in one major and four in the other, he should commence with a 2♣ Stayman bid, attempting to locate an eight-card fit. If he has more than five cards in his major, or if he has a second suit other than a four-card major, he should start by jumping to three of his major suit.

Appropriate actions by responder with a five-card or longer major are as follows.

If responder has 0-5 points   He should bid two of his suit if he has either a singleton or a six-card or longer suit. Otherwise he should pass the opening 1 NT bid.

If responder has 6-7 points

He should bid his long major suit at the two level. This response of 2♡ or 2♠ is a sign off; opener is not allowed to bid further unless he has 18 points and a fit for responder's suit. In the latter event, opener may raise responder's suit to the three level and responder may bid game with 6-7 points.

If responder has 7-9 points and a six-card major

He should jump to game in his suit.

If responder has a hand worth 8-9 points with five cards in one major and fewer than four card in the other major

He should bid 2♣ Stayman. If opener rebids in responder's suit over 2♣, responder can raise to three of the suit to invite game; if opener rebids anything else responder invites game by rebidding his suit on the two level if that is possible (thereby showing a five-card suit), or by rebidding 2 NT if his suit is hearts and opener has rebid 2♠.

If responder has a hand worth 8-9 points with five cards in one major suit and four in the other

He should bid 2♣ Stayman, and if opener bids either major suit, responder should raise to three of that major even if he has five cards in the other major. If opener bids 2◊, responder bids two of his five-card major.

If responder has a hand worth 8-9 points with 5-5 in the major suits

He should again use Stayman. If opener rebids a major over 2♣, responder will raise. If opener rebids 2◇, responder rebids 2♠; and if over 2♠, opener rebids 2 NT, responder can bid 3♡ to show his heart suit as well.

If responder has 10-14 points and a five-card major suit, with or without four cards in the other major, but with no other side suit

He should force to game after starting with 2♣ Stayman. If opener's second bid is in responder's major, responder should bid four of the suit. If opener makes any other second bid, responder should bid three of his suit. *This sequence is forcing to game.* Opener will raise to four with three-card support. If opener's third bid is 3 NT, responder should pass.

If responder has 10-14 points with a six-card major, or with a five-card major and five cards in the other major or four or more cards in a minor

He should jump immediately to three of his major suit. If he has a six-card suit, he should rebid it if opener's second bid is 3 NT. If responders has 5-5 in the major suits, he should jump to 3♠ and rebid 4♡ if opener rebids 3 NT. In either event, if opener's second bid was a raise or responder's suit, responder should pass.

If responder has 15 or more points	He should jump to three of his longest suit, or the higher ranking of his long suits if they are of equal length; over any second bid by opener, responder should bid a new suit.
If responder has a solid six- or seven-card suit with no Aces or Kings outside	He should jump directing to five of his suit. This invites opener to bid six of the suit with a maximum and excellent controls.

Examples:

(a)   ♠ Q x x x x   ♡ x x   ◊ J x x   ♣ x x x

Responder should pass. With one less heart, he should instead bid 2♠.

(b)   ♠ K J x x x   ♡ A x x   ◊ x x   ♣ x x x

Responder should try for game by bidding 2♣ Stayman. If opener rebids 2♠ over 2♣, responder raises to 3♠. If opener rebids anything other than 2♠, responder bids 2♠, showing five spades and 8-9 points.

(c)   ♠ A x x   ♡ K J x x x   ◊ x x   ♣ x x x

Responder should try for game by bidding 2♣ Stayman. If opener rebids 2◊ over 2♣, responder should bid 2♡. If opener rebids 2♡, responder should raise to 3♡. If opener has rebid 2♠, responder should bid 2 NT. Note that responder cannot rebid 3♡ over 2♠ without forcing to game.

When responder rebids 2 NT, opener will not know that responder has five hearts, but will know that he has at least four hearts with 8-9 points.

(d)   ♠ K J x x x   ♡ Q x x   ◇ A J x   ♣ J x

Responder must force to game by bidding 2♣ and then rebidding spades at the three level if opener has not bid 2♠ over 2♣. Responder would jump to 3♠ over a 2◇ or 2♡ rebid by opener.

(e)   ♠ A Q x   ♡ K x x x x   ◇ Q x   ♣ x x x

Responder should force to game by bidding 2♣ and then rebidding hearts at the three level if opener has not rebid 2♡ over 2♣. The three-level rebid is forcing to game.

(f)   ♠ A Q x x x   ♡ x x x   ◇ A K x x   ♣ x

Responder should jump to 3♠.

(g)   ♠ K J x x   ♡ K Q x x x x   ◇ x x   ♣ x

Responder should jump to 3♡. If, instead, he were to bid 2♣ Stayman and locate and play in a 4-4 spade fit, minor suit ruffs might make it difficult to utilize his heart suit.

(h)   ♠ K Q J x x x   ♡ A x x x   ◇ A x   ♣ x

Here, responder should bid 2♣ Stayman despite his six-card spade suit. He has sufficient high card strength to envision a slam and probably enough controls to ensure use of his spades as a side suit if a good 4-4 heart fit is found. Suppose opener had a hand such as:

(i)   ♠ A x   ♡ K Q x x   ◊ J x x   ♣ K Q J x

Against a diamond lead, this hand facing hand (h) would produce a slam only in hearts, not in spades.

(j)   ♠ A K Q J x x x   ♡ x   ◊ Q x   ♣ x x x

Responder should jump to 5♠. This bid implies that he has no high cards with which he could have cue-bid had he shown his suit at a lower level. Opener is asked to bid a slam if he has a maximum with first round control of at least two of the side suits, and at least second round control in the remaining suit.

RESPONSES TO 1 NOTRUMP
IF RESPONDER HOLDS A FIVE-CARD OR LONGER
MINOR SUIT AND NO FOUR-CARD MAJOR

If responder has a hand with a long minor suit and he has *no four-card major suit*, he should generally be content to play the hand in NT. The chief exceptions occur when responder has either a very weak hand or a very strong hand.

With a very weak hand and a six-card suit, responder may sign off in his suit. If his suit is diamonds, he does this simply by bidding 2◊. If his suit is clubs, he cannot sign off in 2♣, because that is the Stayman convention. Thus, he first bids 2♣ and follows by bidding 3♣ over any rebid by opener. Opener will have assumed that the 2♣ bid was Stayman, but will realize from the 3♣ bid that responder has long clubs and intended to sign off. The 3♣ bid is neither forcing nor encouraging.

With a hand worth 15 or more points, or with one worth 10-14 points that contains a singleton or a void, responder should jump to three of his long suit, suggesting a suit contract rather than NT.

Responder's proper actions with a five-card or longer minor suit and no four-card major suit are as follows.

With 0-7 points and long clubs	Responder should bid 2♣, then 3♣.
With 0-7 points and long diamonds	Responder should bid 2♦ with six or more diamonds or with five diamonds and a singleton; otherwise, he should pass.
With 0-7 points with long clubs and long diamonds	Responder should bid 2♦; if opponents then intervene, he should back in by bidding 3♣ with a maximum.
With 6-7 points, with seven or eight clubs or diamonds, and a singleton or void	Responder should bid five of his suit.
With 8-9 points with long clubs or diamonds	Responder should bid 2 NT.
With 8-9 points with 5-4 in minors and no singleton	Responder should bid 2 NT.
With 8-9 points with 5-4 or 5-5 in minors and a three-card major	Responder should bid 2 NT with a weak three-card major suit (no Ace or King); otherwise, he should bid 2♣ intending to raise to three of

the major if opener rebids it over
2♣, or to rebid 2 NT if opener
rebids anything else.

**With 10-14 points with
long clubs or diamonds**

Responder should bid 3 NT if there
is no singleton; otherwise, he
should bid three of the long minor.

**With 15 or more points
with long clubs or
diamonds**

Responder should jump to three of
his suit.

Examples:

(a)   ♠ x x x   ♡ x x   ◊ A J x x x   ♣ x x x

Responder should pass 1 NT.

(b)   ♠ K x   ♡ Q x   ◊ x x x x   ♣ A J x x x

Responder should jump to 3 NT.

(c)   ♠ K x   ♡ x x   ◊ A J x x x   ♣ x x x x

Responder should invite game by bidding 2 NT.

(d)   ♠ K x x   ♡ x x   ◊ x x x x x x   ♣ Q x

*Responder should bid 2 ◊ . This bid is a sign off. Opener is
not allowed to bid further unless he has 18 points and a fit in
diamonds.*

(e)   ♠ K x x   ♡ x   ◊ Q x x   ♣ x x x x x x

Responder should sign off in clubs, by bidding 2♣ followed by 3♣.

(f)   ♠ Q x x   ♡ x x   ◊ J x   ♣ K J 10 x x x

Responder should make a game try by raising to 2 NT.

(g)   ♠ K x x   ♡ x   ◊ A Q x x x x   ♣ K x x

Responder should jump to 3 ◊ ; his suit is good and, opposite an appropriate opening such as ♠ A J x ♡ A x x ◊ K x ♣ A J x x his hand should produce eleven or twelve tricks in diamonds.

(h)   ♠ Q x   ♡ x x x   ◊ A J 10 x x x x   ♣ x

Does not offer good prospects for eleven tricks, and responder should jump to 3 NT. If responder had one more diamond he would jump to 5 ◊ instead of 3 NT.

(i)   ♠ K x x   ♡ x   ◊ K x x   ♣ K J x x x x

Presents the obvious danger that the opponents would run the heart suit against a 3 NT contract. Responder's best bid is 2♣ Stayman. If opener rebids 2♠, responder can raise to game in spades, playing in the 4-3 trump fit, with his own shorter trump holding available to ruff hearts. If opener rebids 2♡, responder can try 3 NT with a greater feeling of security since opener will have Q x x x or better in hearts (opener could, of course, bid 4♠ over 3 NT if he had four spades as well as four hearts). If opener rebids 2 ◊ , responder can try jumping to 5♣ knowing that opener has 7 or 8 cards in the minor suits.

(j)   ♠ J x x   ♡ x   ◇ A K x x   ♣ Q x x x x

Despite the danger that the opponents would run the heart suit against a 3 NT contract, responder's spade holding here is not strong enough to risk a four-spade contract. Thus, responder should jump to 3 NT and hope for the best.

ONE NOTRUMP OPENER'S SECOND BID

The opening NT bid having narrowly defined opener's hand in terms of strength and distribution, opener's rebids are briefly spelled out in light of responder's first bid.

OPENER'S SECOND BID
AFTER RESPONDER HAS BID 2♣ STAYMAN

Over a 2♣ Stayman response opener must show a biddable (Q x x x or better) four-card major suit if he has one.

With four hearts	He rebids 2♡ .
With four spades	He rebids 2♠
With four hearts and four spades	He rebids 2♡ .
With no biddable four-card major suit	He rebids 2◇ .

No other rebids are available to opener over a 2♣ Stayman response.

OPENER'S SECOND BID
AFTER RESPONDER HAS BID 2 ♦, 2 ♥, OR 2 ♠

The responses of 2 ♦, 2 ♥, and 2 ♠ are sign offs. Opener must pass, unless he has a maximum and a fit for responder's suit.

If he has at least three cards headed by a high honor in responder's suit and 18 points, opener may raise responder's suit to the three level.

If responder's suit is diamonds, opener may, alternatively, rebid 2 NT if he has all suits guarded.

OPENER'S SECOND BID
AFTER RESPONDER HAS RAISED TO 2 NOTRUMP

This response invites game in NT. Opener should rebid 3 NT with 17 or 18 points. With 16 points he should pass.

OPENER'S SECOND BID
AFTER RESPONDER HAS BID 3 ♣, 3 ♦, 3 ♥, OR 3 ♠

These responses are game forcing slam tries.

If opener has a fit for responder's suit and a hand rich in Aces and Kings rather than in Queens and Jacks, he should bid a new suit—a cue-bid. This cue-bid encourages responder to explore further.

Without a fit for responder's suit, or with a hand laden with Queens and Jacks, opener should rebid 3 NT.

Examples:

(a)   ♠ K J x   ♥ A Q x x   ♦ A x x x   ♣ Q x

Opener should cue-bid in the suit of his cheapest Ace if responder makes a slam try in diamonds, hearts, or spades. If responder has bid 3◊, opener should cue-bid 3♡. If responder has bid 3♡ or 3♠, opener should bid 4◊. If responder bids 3♣, opener should sign off with 3 NT.

(b)   ♠ K Q x   ♡ Q J x x   ◊ K Q J x   ♣ A x

This hand lacks Aces. Thus, even though it has two more high card points than hand (a), opener should merely bid game over responder's jump: 3 NT over 3♣ or 3◊; 4♡ over 3♡; or 4♠ over 3♠.

OPENER'S SECOND BID
AFTER RESPONDER HAS RAISED TO 3 NOTRUMP

This response is a sign off. Opener should not bid further.

OPENER'S SECOND BID AFTER RESPONDER HAS BID 4♣

This response is the Gerber convention, asking opener how many Aces he has. (See page 000).

OPENER'S SECOND BID AFTER RESPONDER HAS BID 4◊

This response has no standard meaning. Opener should not pass. It may be that responder intends to jump at his next turn to 6 NT, suggesting that he had 19-20 high card points, enough to guarantee a small slam and to invite a grand slam.

Probably the best move is for opener to cue-bid a major suit Ace if he has one, or to rebid 4 NT without one. Since the 4 ◊ response has no standard meaning, however, it is probably immaterial what action opener takes so long as he does not pass.

OPENER'S SECOND BID
AFTER RESPONDER HAS BID 4♡ OR 4♠

These responses promise six-card or longer suits with less than 10 points. They are sign offs. Opener should not bid further.

OPENER'S SECOND BID
AFTER RESPONDER HAS RAISED TO 4 NOTRUMP

This response asks opener to bid a small slam with a maximum, otherwise to pass.

Opener should bid 6 NT, if he has 18 points or a good 17; with 16 or a bad 17, he should pass. A "good" 17 would consist principally of Aces and Kings, with any Queen or Jack being in combination with an Ace or King.

OPENER'S SECOND BID
AFTER RESPONDER HAS BID 5♣ OR 5◊

These responses normally show broken seven- or eight-card suits and very unbalanced hands, containing at least one singleton or void.

Opener should pass, unless he has a good fit for responder's suit, first round control of two side suits and solid second round control in the other side suit, with reason to believe that twelve tricks can be made. With such a hand, opener may raise responder's suit to six.

OPENER'S SECOND BID
AFTER RESPONDER HAS BID 5♡ OR 5♠

These responses show slam tries with a solid six-card or longer suit, but no outside Aces (for otherwise responder would jump to three of his suit and then cue-bid).

In order to raise, opener should have at least two Aces and at least the King of any side suit in which he does not have the Ace, and prospects for taking four-five tricks in his own hand.

If opener wants to be in slam and has significant tenace positions, he should bid 6 NT rather than six of responder's suit.

OPENER'S SECOND BID
AFTER RESPONDER HAS RAISED TO 5 NOTRUMP

This response shows 19-20 high card points. It forces opener to bid a small slam and invites a grand slam.

If opener has 18 points or a good 17, he should bid 7 NT; with 16 or a bad 17, he should rebid 6 NT.

OPENER'S SECOND BID AFTER
RESPONDER HAS BID SIX OF A SUIT OR 6 NOTRUMP

These responses show 17-18 points and indicate that responder believes a small slam can be made in the denomination he has bid, but that a grand slam is doubtful. Opener is not invited to bid further.

NOTRUMP OPENER'S SECOND BID
AFTER RESPONDER HAS PASSED

If responder has passed and the opponents have kept the bidding alive, opener should not bid again unless he has opened 1 NT on an unusual hand.

MEANINGS OF
RESPONSES AND REBIDS AFTER
AN OPPONENT HAS OVERCALLED

After an opening bid of 1 NT has been overcalled, responses at the two and three level retain their original meanings; two level responses are not forcing; three level responses are forcing.

Responder's invitational options, however, are severly limited by the overcall because he is precluded from using the 2♣ response as Stayman. His only invitational call is thus 2 NT, promising 8-9 points and not necessarily showing a stopper in the suit overcalled.

With a hand worth 10 points or more with which he does not know in what denomination to play, responder may cue-bid the suit overcalled. Opener will bid a four-card major if he has one, or will bid 3 NT with a stopper in the suit overcalled, or a four- card minor suit if he has neither of the above.

If 1 NT has been opened and the Stayman 2♣ response has been made and is followed by an overcall, opener should bid a four-card major suit if he has one; otherwise, he should pass.

RESPONSES TO
HIGHER NOTRUMP OPENINGS

Openings of 2 NT or higher promise great strength. However, the higher the level of the openings, the less room responder has to explore exactly how high and in what denomination the hand should be played.

When considering slam, responder, should avoid showing suits that lack the top honors. Slam hands with weak suits (i.e., not headed by at least the Queen; should generally be steered into NT. Length points should not be counted for weak suits.

RESPONSES TO OPENING OF 2 NOTRUMP

Opposite an opening of 2 NT, which promises 22-24 points, any response is forcing to game.

Most suit responses promise five or more cards in the suit bid. A 3♣ response is the Stayman convention, asking opener to bid a four-card major suit if he has one. A 4♣ response to 2 NT is the Gerber convention, asking opener how many Aces he has.

In general, responder should set his sights as follows.

With 0-3 points   Pass.

With 4-8 points   Settle for game.

With 9-10 points   Try for small slam by an eventual bid of 4 NT or five of a major suit.

With 11-12 points   Bid small slam.

With 13-14 points	Try for grand slam by an eventual bid of 5 NT. Such a bid forces opener to bid at least a small slam.
With 15-18 points	Bid grand slam.

Responder should take the following initial actions over 2 NT if he has 4 or more points.

With no four-card major, and either a balanced hand or one whose only long suit is clubs	Responder should bid NT at the appropriate level for his strength (3 NT with 4-8 points, 4 NT with 9-10 points, 6 NT with 11-12 points, 5 NT with 13-14 points, or 7 NT with 15-18 points).
With four hearts and/or four spades, and other than 4-3-3-3 distribution	Responder should bid 3♣ Stayman. If opener's second bid is in responder's major, responder raises that suit to the appropriate level for his strength (to four with 4-8 points, to five with 9-10 points, to six with 11-12 points, or to seven with 15-18 points (with 13-14 points, responder bids 5 NT). If opener's second bid is not in responder's major, responder should bid NT at the appropriate level for his strength.
With a five-card major and a four-card major	Responder should bid 3♣ Stayman. If opener's second bid is in a major, responder raises that major (even if he

has five cards in the other major) to the appropriate level for his strength.

If opener's second bid is 3◇, responder bids three of his five-card major. If opener raises to four (showing three-card support), responder passes with 4-8 points, or raises the suit to the appropriate level with greater strength.

If opener's third bid is 3 NT, showing a doubleton in responder's suit, responder passes with 4-8 points, or raises in NT to the appropriate level with greater strength.

With a five-card major and fewer than four cards in the other major

Responder should bid three of his major. If opener raises to four, responder passes with 4-8 points, or raises the suit to the appropriate level with greater strength. If opener's second bid is 3 NT, responder passes with 4-8 points, or raises in NT to the appropriate level with greater strength.

With a six-card or longer major

With 4-8 points, responder should bid three of his suit. If opener raises to four, responder should pass. If opener's second bid is 3 NT, responder should bid four of his suit.

With 9 points, responder should jump directly to four of his suit. *The jump to four is a mild slam try.* With 10 points, responder should jump to five of his suit. *The jump to five is a strong slam try.* With 11-12 points, responder should bid six of his suit if it is a good suit; if his suit is weakish (headed by the Jack or 10), responder should start by bidding three of his suit. If opener raises, responder should bid six of the suit; if opener's second bid is 3 NT, showing a doubleton in the suit, responder's second bid should be five of his suit, instructing opener to take his choice between six of the suit and 6 NT.

With five cards in each major, or with six cards in each major, or with six spades and five hearts

Responder should bid 3♠. If he has 4-8 points, he should pass if opener bids 4♠, or bid 4♡ if opener bids 3 NT. With more than 8 points, responder should, over either a 3 NT or a 4♠ rebid by opener, bid 5♡ with 9-10 points, or 6♡ with 11-12 points. If opener has more hearts than spades, he will place the contract in hearts; otherwise he will return to spades. Over responder's 5♡ bid, opener will bid the suit of his choice at the six level.

With six hearts and five spades

Responder should bid 3♡. If he has 4-8 points, he should pass if opener bids 4♡, or bid 4♡ if opener's second bid is 3 NT. With more than 8 points, responder should bid spades at his second turn: 4♠ with 9-10 points, or 5♠ with 11-12 points. *Both the 4♠ and the 5♠ rebid by responder are forcing.*

With six or more diamonds

With 4-8 points, responder should bid 3 NT unless he has at least a seven- card suit which is quite broken; in the latter circumstances, he should jump to 5 ◊. With 9-10 points, responder should bid 4 NT if he has no singleton, or 3 ◊ if he has a singleton. *The 3 ◊ response is itself a mild slam try;* if opener's second bid is 3 NT, responer should pass with 9 points, or bid 4 ◊ with a good 10 points. With 11-12 points and a good suit, responder should jump to 6 ◊ with a singleton, or 6 NT without a singleton; with a weakish suit, responder should bid 3 ◊ followed by 5 ◊.

With six or more clubs

Responder should bid NT at the appropriate level for his strength unless he has either 4-8 points with a broken seven-card suit, or 11-12 points with a good suit and a side singleton. In the former case, responder should jump to 5 ♣. In the latter case, he should jump to 6 ♣.

With nine or more cards in two suits, other than hearts-spades

With 4-8 points, responder should bid 3 NT if he does not have a four-card or longer major suit. With 9 or more points, responder should bid both of his suits, bidding the higher ranking one first if they are of equal length, or if unequal, bidding the longer first.

Examples (After a 2 NT opening):

(a) ♠ J x x x x x   ♡ x x   ◊ x x   ♣ x x x

Responder should pass.

(b) ♠ Q J x x   ♡ A x x   ◊ x x x   ♣ K x x

Responder should jump to 4 NT.

(c) ♠ x x   ♡ K J x x x x   ◊ x x x   ♣ x x

Responder should bid 3♡. If opener bids 4♡, responder should pass. If opener bids 3 NT, responder should bid 4♡.

(d) ♠ x x   ♡ A K x x x x   ◊ x x   ♣ x x x

Responder should jumpt to 4♡. This is a mild slam try.

(e) ♠ x   ♡ K J x x x x   ◊ Q x x x   ♣ K J

Responder should plan to bid 6♡. However, before doing so, he should bid 4♣, Gerber, to be sure that the partnership is not missing two Aces.

(f) ♠ K x   ♡ x   ◊ J x x x x x   ♣ x x x

Responder should jump to 5◊.

(g) ♠ x x   ♡ x   ◊ K Q x x x x   ♣ x x x

Responder should bid 3 NT.

(h) ♠ K x x x   ♡ x x   ◊ A J x x   ♣ Q J x

Responder should bid 3♣ Stayman. If opener bids 3♠, re-

sponder should jump to 6♠; if opener bids 3◇ or 3♡, responder should jump to 6 NT.

RESPONSES TO OPENING OF 3 NOTRUMP

Opposite a 3 NT opening, which shows 25-27 points, responder may sign off in any game, may conduct very limited exploration for a major suit game, and may invite slam.

Bids other than 4♣ or 4◇ promise six or more cards in the suit bid. A response of 4♣ is the Gerber convention, asking opener how many Aces he has. A response of 4◇ to 3 NT is the Stayman convention, asking opener to bid a four-card major suit if he has one.

In general, responder should set his sights as follows:

With 0-5 points	Pass or bid game in any suit.
With 6-7 points	Try for small slam.
With 8-9 points	Bid small slam.
With 10-11 points	Try for grand slam.
With 12 or more points	Bid grand slam.

In response to a 3 NT opening, responder should take the following initial actions.

With a six-card or longer major suit	Responder should bid four of his suit with 0-5 points, or five of his suit with 6-7 points. With 8-9 points, responder should use the Gerber convention to determine that the partnership is not missing two Aces, before bidding six of

his suit. With 10-11 points, responder should jump to six of his suit without using Gerber. This is a mild invitation to opener to bid a grand slam with a maximum.

With a six-card or longer minor suit

With 0-5 points, responder should bid five of his minor if he has a broken seven-card or longer suit; otherwise, he should pass 3 NT. With 6-7 points, he should bid 4 NT. With 8-9 points, responder should bid six of his suit after using the Gerber convention to determine that the partnership is not missing two Aces. With 10-11 points, responder should jump directly to six of his suit. This jump is a grand slam try.

With four or five cards in a major suit

Responder should bid 4 ◊ Stayman. If opener rebids in responder's major, responder will pass with 0-5 points, raise to five with 6-7 points, or raise to six with 8-9 points, or bid 5 NT with 10-11 points. If responder has 0-5 points, he should pass if opener rebids 4 NT. If opener rebids 4 ♡ and responder has five spades, responder's second bid with 0-5 points should be 4 ♠.

If responder has more than 5 points, and opener has not rebid in responder's major suit, responder bids a new suit at the five level with 6-7 points, at the six level with 8-9 points; or bids 5 NT with 10-11 points.

| With any other distribution | Responder passes with 0-5 points, or raises to 4 NT with 6-7 points, to 5 NT with 10-11 points, to 6 NT with 8-9 points, or to 7 NT with 12-15 points. |

RESPONSES TO OPENING OF 4 NOTRUMP

Any response to a 4 NT opening bid, which promises 28-29 points, invites opener to bid a small slam with 29 points.

Because of the height at which the auction has started, the only way in which responder can invite a small slam in NT is by bidding 5 NT. There are no bids available with which to force to a small slam while inviting a grand slam.

In response to a 4 NT opening, responder should take the following actions.

With any distribution and 0-3 points	Responder should pass.
With a six-card or longer suit	Responder should bid five of his suit with 4-5 points. With 6-8 points, he should bid six of his suit if he has a singleton, or 6 NT without a singleton. With 9-12 points, he should jump to seven of his suit with a singleton, or 7 NT with no singleton.
With no six-card or longer suit	Responder should bid 5 NT with 4-5 points, 6 NT with 6-8 points, or 7 NT with 9-12 points.

RESPONSES TO OPENING OF 5 NOTRUMP

The opening bid of 5 NT does not show a precise point count, but merely guarantees that opener can take eleven tricks in his own hand. Responder should raise to 6 NT if he has an Ace or a King or a Queen, or raise to 7 NT if he has two such cards.

RESPONSES TO OPENING OF 6 NOTRUMP

The opening of 6 NT does not show a precise count, but guarantees that the opener can take 12 tricks in his own hand. Responder should raise to seven if he has either an Ace or a King.

SUMMARY OF RESPONSES TO NOTRUMP OPENINGS

	Points Opposite 1 NT Opening (16 to 18)	Points Opposite 2 NT Opening (22 to 24)	Points Opposite 3 NT Opening (25 to 27)	Points Opposite 4 NT Opening (28 to 29)
Sign Off	0 to 7	0 to 3	0 to 5	0 to 3
Try for Game	8 to 9	—	—	—
Force to Game	10 to 14	4 to 8	—	—
Try for Small Slam	15 to 16	9 to 10	6 to 7	4 to 5
Force to Small Slam	17 to 18	11 to 12	8 to 9	6 to 8
Try for Grand Slam	19 to 20	13 to 14	10 to 11	—
Bid Grand Slam	21 to 24	15 to 18	12 to 15	9 to 12

One-Level Suit Openings and Sequences

OPENING 1 OF A SUIT

Any hand not suitable for a NT opening must, if it is to be opened at all, be opened in a suit.

A NT opening may be inappropriate for any of three reasons:

(a) Wrong strength (for example, 19-21 high card points).

(b) Wrong distribution (for example, singleton).

(c) Wrong suit texture (for example, two suits unguarded). Thus, opening bids in a suit cover a very wide variety of hands.

The only opening bids to which responder is required to respond are openings in two of a suit. No other opening bids are forcing.

MINIMUM STRENGTH FOR OPENING ONE IN A SUIT

A player is allowed to open with one of a suit if he has as little as 13 points, counting both high cards and distribution. With 14 or more points, he is required to open.

Whether or not a player chooses to open with 13 points depends in part on whether or not he has two or more defensive tricks and whether or not his high cards are concentrated in his long suits. His choice also depends on whether or not he will have an appropriate rebid, since if responder has not previously passed, and responds in a new suit, opener is forced to rebid.

Examples:

(a)   ♠ Q x x x x   ♡ K Q J x   ◊ K x   ♣ x x

Worth 13 points, counting 11 in high cards and 2 for distribution. Should not be opened because it contains only 1½ defensive tricks.

(b)   ♠ x x x x x   ♡ x x x x   ◊ K Q   ♣ A Q

Contains 2½ defensive tricks and 13 points. However, should not be opened because the honor cards are poorly located in the short suits.

(c)   ♠ A Q x x x   ♡ K Q x x   ◊ x x   ♣ x x

With the same high cards and suit distribution as hand (b), this hand should be opened because the high cards are usefully situated.

(d)   ♠ A Q x x x x   ♡ x   ◊ A J x x   ♣ x x

A mandatory opening with a total of 14 points.

(e)   ♠ A Q x   ♡ J x x x   ◇ A Q x   ♣ x x x

Should not be opened despite its three defensive tricks and 13 points because it would not provide an appropriate rebid if responder were to respond 2♣ or 2◇.

MAXIMUM STRENGTH FOR OPENING ONE IN A SUIT

The opening bid of one of a suit is not forcing. Consequently, with a strong hand that is close to producing a game on its own, the bidding should not be opened at the one level.

Examples:

(a)   ♠ A x x   ♡ A K Q J x x x   ◇ A x x   ♣ —

Will produce nine tricks on its own and should be opened with 2♡, not 1♡.

(b)   ♠ A Q J x x   ♡ A K x x x   ◇ A K   ♣ x

Should be opened with 2♠, with the intention of rebidding hearts.

(c)   ♠ A K x x   ♡ x   ◇ A K x x   ♣ A K x x

Although it has the same number of high card points as hand (b), and more high card points than hand (a), this hand does not offer the reasonable expectation of winning nine tricks on its own. It should be opened with 1♣, intending to make a strong rebid if responder responds.

SUIT TEXTURE REQUIRED FOR
OPENING BID OF ONE IN A SUIT

A major suit is biddable as an opening bid if it is four cards long and is headed by at least the Queen and Jack.

Any five-card suit is biddable regardless of its texture.

A minor suit is biddable it it is four cards long, regardless of its texture. A minor is also biddable as an opening bid—if necessary for the appropriate rebidding of the hand—if it is three cards long, and preferably headed by the Ace, King or Queen.

Examples:

(a)   ♠ Q x x x   ♡ x   ◇ x x x x   ♣ A K Q x

The spade suit is not biddable, but both diamonds and clubs are biddable.

(b)   ♠ x x x x x   ♡ A K x x   ◇ A x   ♣ x x

Both the spade and heart suits are biddable.

(c)   ♠ Q x x x   ♡ Q x x x   ◇ Q J x   ♣ A K

Neither hearts nor spades are biddable. The hand must be opened (the 14 high card points make the opening mandatory) with 1 ◇ , the three-card minor suit.

SELECTING WHICH SUIT TO OPEN

Finding a biddable suit is only a small part of the job of deciding which suit to open. Even before making his first bid, opener must think ahead to his next bid, for he must be prepared to make a rebid that is consistent with the length and texture of his suits and the strength of his hand.

If opener has one suit that is longer than each of the others, he should generally open the long suit. This is true even though there may be more high card strength in the shorter suits than in the long suit.

Examples:

(a)   ♠ A K x   ♡ K x x x x   ◊ A x x   ♣ x x

Should be opened with 1 ♡.

(b)   ♠ x   ♡ A K x x x   ◊ x   ♣ K Q J x x x

Should be opened with 1 ♣.

(c)   ♠ x   ♡ A Q J x x x   ◊ x   ♣ K Q x x x

Should be opened with 1 ♡.

There are a few exceptions to this rule, influenced chiefly by the principle of preparedness. The principle of preparedness dictates that a player not open the bidding in a certain suit

—if he will have to rebid in this suit and the suit is worse than five cards headed by the Queen and Jack (note that it is permissible to rebid any six-card suit, regardless of its texture);

—or if this choice will force him, to make his second bid at the three level with less than 17 points, or to make a rebid of 2 NT with less than 15 points;

—or if this choice will force him, with less than 19 points, to make his second bid at the two level in a suit that ranks higher than his first suit (this sequence of bidding is called a "reverse").

Examples:

    (d)   ♠ A K x x   ♡ x x x   ◇ A J x   ♣ Q x x

If the bidding is opened in the "long" suit, spades, opener will have insuperable rebid problems if responder bids any new suit. Thus, he should make the "prepared" opening of 1♣.

    (e)   ♠ A Q x x   ♡ x x x x x   ◇ K x   ♣ A x

Opener's heart suit is biddable, but is not rebiddable. Thus, if he were to open 1♡ and the response were 2♣ or 2◇, he would not be able to rebid 2♡. Nor could he rebid 2♠, since this would be a reverse, showing 19+ points. This hand should therefore be opened 1♠ rather than 1♡.

OPENING WHEN HOLDING TWO SUITS, EACH CONTAINING FIVE OR MORE CARDS

With two long suits of equal length, that is, two five-card suits or two six-card suits, opener should open the higher ranking suit, planning to rebid twice in the lower ranking suit.

Examples:

    (a)   ♠ K Q J x x   ♡ K x x x x   ◇ A x   ♣ x

The opening bid should be 1♠, and the rebid should be in hearts.

    (b)   ♠ x   ♡ A K x x x x   ◇ —   ♣ K Q J x x x

The bidding should be opened 1♡, with clubs being rebid.

With suits of unequal length—6-5 or 7-6—opener should open the longer suit, then bid and rebid the shorter suit. This may involve a reverse when opener's longer suit ranks lower than his shorter suit, but 6-5 or more freakish distribution makes up for any lack of high card points. When opener makes his second rebid showing 6-5, responder will know not to count on opener for a hand that is powerful in high cards.

Opener's rebids help to clarify for responder how many cards opener has in each of his two suits.

If opener opens in one suit and then bids and rebids another suit without support from responder, he promises at least five cards in his second suit.

Since opener's first suit in such an auction cannot be shorter than his second suit, he must have at least five carts in his first suit also. If his first suit ranks higher than his second, the first suit might have five, six, or seven cards. But if the suit opened is lower in rank than the suit rebid, the suit opened must be longer than the second suit, in other words, six or seven cards.

Examples:

(c)   ♠ K Q x x x   ♡ x   ◊ A Q x x x x   ♣ x

Opener would open with 1◊, and then bid and rebid spades, showing five spades and at least six diamonds.

(d)   ♠ x   ♡ A K x x x x   ◊ x   ♣ A Q x x x

Opener would open with 1♡, then bid and rebid clubs. Responder will know that opener has five or more clubs and at least as many hearts as clubs. His exact heart-club distribution, however could be 6-6, as in hand (b) above, or 6-5 as in hand (d), or 5-5.

OPENING WHEN HOLDING
A 4-CARD AND A 5-CARD SUIT

When opener has a rebiddable five-card suit and a four-card suit, he should generally open the five-card suit. In this way, opener will have a comfortable rebid, either in his second suit or in his first suit—over all expected responses. If the five-card suit is not a rebiddable suit, it should be treated as a four-card suit and the rules stated for showing two four-card suits should be followed.

The one exception to the principle that the longer, rebiddable, suit should be opened occurs when the four-card suit is strong and ranks just above the five-card suit and the hand is worth less than 19 points. In this circumstance, opener should open the four-card suit and rebid the five-card suit.

Examples:

(a)   ♠ A J x x x   ♡ x x   ◊ K Q x x   ♣ Q x

Opener should open 1♠; he can rebid 2◊ over a 2♣ response or 2♠ over a 2♡ response.

(b)   ♠ x x x x x   ♡ A x   ◊ A Q x x   ♣ K x

The spade suit is not rebiddable; opener should open 1◊, planning to rebid 1♠.

(c)   ♠ x x   ♡ K Q J x   ◊ K x   ♣ A x x x x

Should be opened with 1♣; over a 1◊ response opener can rebid 1♡; or over a 1♠ response he can rebid 1 NT.

(d)   ♠ A x x x   ♡ K Q J x x   ◊ K x   ♣ x x

Opener should open 1♡ planning to rebid hearts over a 2♣ or 2◊ response.

(e)   ♠ A Q J x   ♡ K x x x x   ◊ K x   ♣ x x

Opener's spade suit here is stronger than in hand (d). He should show both of his suits. He should open 1♠ and rebid 2♡.

OPENING WHEN HOLDING TWO 4-CARD SUITS

With a minimum hand, opener must be careful not to bid his suits in such an order that responder cannot return to opener's first suit at the two level. With a strong hand, worth 19-21 points, opener should try to avoid opening with a major suit, which would make it more difficult for responder to respond with a marginal hand.

When opener's two four-card suits are adjacent to one another, that is, spades and hearts, or hearts and diamonds, or diamonds and clubs, the higher ranking suit should be opened. The only exception would be for a very strong hand such as:

Example:

(a)   ♠ A J x x   ♡ A K x x   ◊ A x x   ♣ K J.

With so strong a hand, opener should avoid opening 1♠, and should open either 1♡ or 1◊, hoping that responder can respond so that opener will have an opportunity to make a jump rebid showing his strength.

When opener's two four-card suits are not adjacent to one another, there are three possibilities: he has either clubs and spades, or clubs and hearts, or diamonds and spades.

With four clubs and four spades and a hand of any strength, opener should start with 1♣ in order to be able to show both of his suits at a low level. If responder bids either 1◊ or 1♡ in response to

1♣, opener can rebid 1♠ with any hand worth less than 20 points. If instead he opened with 1♠, and responder bid at the two level, opener could not show his clubs below the three level, which would require at least 17 points.

With four clubs and four hearts, opener similarly should open with 1♣ because his rebid problems with a less-than 19 point hand will be easier. He can rebid 1♡ over a response of 1◇, or 1 NT over a response of 1♠. If instead he opened with 1♡, he would have no convenient rebid over a 2◇ response unless he had 15-18 points and the stoppers required to bid 2 NT.

With four diamonds and four spades and a hand worth less than 19 points, opener should open the suit that ranks below his doubleton. Since the response is more likely to be in the suit in which opener has fewest cards, adherence to this principle solves most of the rebid problems.

Examples:

(b)   ♠ A K x x   ♡ x x x   ◇ A Q x x   ♣ x x

A 1♠ opening is appropriate; for the purpose of determining with which suit to open the bidding, spades are deemed to rank next below clubs. After a 1♠ opening, opener has an adequate rebid over any response: 2◇ over a 2♣ response, or 3♡ over a 2♡ response.

(c)   ♠ A K x x   ♡ x x   ◇ A Q x x   ♣ x x x

1◇, the suit below the doubleton, should be opened. If the hand were opened with 1♠ and the response were 2♡, opener would have no appropriate rebid. After a 1◇ opening, opener has a convenient 1♠ rebid after the expected 1♡ response. Of course, after the less likely response of 2♣, opener does not have a good rebid, and will be forced to re-

bid his diamond suit even though it lacks a fifth card; this is preferable to showing greater strength than he has by bidding 2♠ (a reverse), or 3♣, or 2 NT. A 2 NT rebid, in addition to showing extra strength, would promise a heart stopper which opener does not have.

OPENING WHEN HOLDING THREE 4-CARD SUITS

When the hand contains three four-card suits, it is normally best to open in the suit ranking just below the singleton. For these purposes, spades are considered to rank below clubs. Since the suit in which partner is most likely to respond is the one in which opener is shortest, opening in the suit below the singleton makes rebidding convenient.

Examples:

(a)   ♠ A Q x x   ♡ x   ◇ K Q x x   ♣ J x x x

Should be opened with 1◇; over the anticipated 1♡ response, opener can rebid 1♠.

(b)   ♠ K Q x x   ♡ A x x x   ◇ K J x x   ♣ x

The bidding should be opened with 1♠; after a 2♣ response, opener can rebid 2♡, and perhaps rebid his diamonds later. After a 2◇ response, opener can rebid 2♡. After a 2♡ response, opener can raise to 3♡.

When opener has a very strong hand with three four-card suits, it is normally best to open in the lowest ranking four-card suit in order to make it easier for partner to respond.

Example:

(c)   ♠AKxx   ♡x   ◊AKxx   ♣AQxx

This hand should be opened 1♣.

RESPONSES TO
AN OPENING BID OF 1 IN A SUIT

The rules that follow assume that neither opponent has entered the auction.

When the opening bid has been one of a suit, responder must bear in mind that the strength of the opener's hand can range from 13 to 21 points.

Opener's distribution may be either balanced or unbalanced.

Responder should assume that opener has 13-15 points, and should base any action on that premise, until contrary evidence appears.

Responder must also cater to the possibility that opener may hold as many as 21 points.

When contemplating a final contract in NT, responder should count only his high card points plus points for extra cards in his long suits.

When contemplating a final contract in a suit, responder should count his high card points and points for the ruffing value of his short suits, assuming he has enough trumps for ruffing. Normally the partnership should try to name as trumps a suit in which they hold a total of eight or more cards.

HOW HIGH RESPONDER SHOULD AIM

Bearing in mind that the partnership should reach game with 26 points, slam with 33 points, and a grand slam with 37 points, responder should conduct himself as follows after an opening in a suit.

0-5 points   Pass.

6-10 points   Keep the bidding open. Responder should not count on being able to bid more than once with a hand of this strength.

11-12 points   Try for game. Responder may bid twice with a hand of this strength, even if opener does not make an encouraging rebid.

13-16 points   Force to game.

17-19 points   Try for slam.

20 or more   Force to slam.
points

RESPONSES THAT ARE FORCING

Any bid of a new suit by responder is forcing, if he has not already passed during the auction. This response is forcing only for one round and not to game. That is, opener is required to rebid once, and must await further action by responder in order to know if he is required to bid a third time.

Any single jump by responder, whether in opener's suit, or in a new suit, or in NT, is forcing. These responses are forcing to game.

That is, opener is required to continue bidding until game is reached.

Jumps by responder to 4 NT (Blackwood) or to 5 NT (Grand Slam Force) are conventional slam tries. Each of these bids forces opener to give specific information.

EFFECT OF RESPONDER'S HAVING PASSED ORIGINALLY

If responder has had an opportunity to open the bidding and has failed to do so, he cannot have a hand worth 14 or more points, and rarely has one worth 13. **Thus, there is no response that such a responder can make that is forcing to game.**

A jump by responder in opener's suit or in a new suit or in NT therefore becomes an invitation to game.

If responder is a passed hand, a non-jump response in a new suit, no longer forces opener to rebid.

Opener will frequently rebid when the new suit response has been at the one level, but will often pass when the response has been at the two level.

RESPONSES THAT ARE NOT FORCING

The following responses to an opening bid of one of a suit are not forcing.

1 NT	Shows 6-9 points and suggests balanced distribution.
Raise to two of opener's suit	Shows 6-9 points and at least three-card support for opener's suit.

Any bid of exactly game	These responses range in high card strength from the fairly weak (game raise of opener's suit with less than 10 points) to the fairly strong (jump to 3 NT with 16-18 high card points).
Any bid of slam	When made immediately, such a response promises great playing strength.
Raise to five of opener's major suit	Invites opener to bid a small slam if he has two of the top three honors in his suit. Otherwise, opener is to pass.
Double or triple jumps by responder in a new suit (for example, after 1 ♡ by opener, 3 ♠ , 4 ♣, 4 ◇ , 4 ♠ , 5 ♣ , 5 ◇ by responder)	These responses are pre-emptive and are based on a long suit in responder's hand, but little high card strength.

While all of the above bids are non-forcing, opener is not forbidden to bid again. The non-forcing responses are predicated on the minimum hand opener can have. If opener has a special hand, he may rebid over a non-forcing response.

RESPONSES THAT ARE GAME INVITATIONAL

In standard bidding, if responder is not a passed hand, there are no first round responses in NT or in opener's suit that are in and of themselves invitations to game.

The only first round bids by responder that constitute game invitations are non-jump bids in a new suit at the two level.

If responder has a hand that is valued at 11-12 points but must make his first bid in a new suit at the one level, he must make an encouraging *rebid* in order to invite game.

Examples:

(a)   ♠ x x   ♡ A x x   ◇ K Q J x x   ♣ x x x

Over an opening of 1♡ or 1♠, responder will bid 2◇, showing at least 10 points, or game invitation strength.

(b)   ♠ A x x x   ♡ x x   ◇ K Q J x   ♣ J x x

Over an opening of 1♡, responder will bid 1♠ which does not promise more than 6 points. Responder will have to bid a new suit at his next turn to show a hand worth a game invitation.

RAISES OF OPENER'S SUIT

An immediate raise of opener's suit promises reasonably good trump support. Usually responder has at least four cards in opener's suit. For a raise to the two level, responder may have only three card support of any texture if he holds a singleton or doubleton in a side suit, and can find no more suitable bid.

The trump support needed for an immediate raise is as follows:

If the opening bid has been 1♡ or 1♠	An immediate raise to three—forcing to game—promises at least four cards in opener's suit. This bid suggests that

responder has no good five-card side suit: since the force to game invites slam exploration, it is to be inferred that responder would have shown a good five-card suit before raising if he had one.

An immediate raise to four shows long trumps and a singleton or void in some side suit, but little high card strength. For such a raise, responder should have less than 10 high card points.

If the opening bid has been 1♣ or 1♢

Any raise by responder promises at least four trumps and indicates that responder has no good four-card major.

For a raise to the four or five level, responder's hand should be wildly distributional since he bypasses 3 NT, the 9-trick game, to make this jump.

The strength needed for an immediate raise is as follows:

Single raise (e.g., 1♠ to 2♠)   6-9 points.

Double raise (e.g., 1♢ to 3♢)   13-15 points.

Triple raise (e.g., 1♡ to 4♡)   Less than 10 high card points.

Quadruple raise in minor (e.g., 1♢ to 5♢)   Less than 10 high card points.

Quadruple raise in major (e.g., 1♡ to 5♡)

Playing power with side suits controlled, needing only good trumps from opener to make a slam.

Quintuple raise (e.g., 1♠ to 6♠, or 1♣ to 6♣)

Great playing power, but undoubtedly the hand includes a void, and perhaps a weak doubleton in a side suit. Bidding a slam in this way is called "blasting," and is done in the hope that if there is a lead to defeat the slam, this auction will give the opponents the least opportunity to find it.

Responder will sometimes have a hand with which he wants to play in opener's suit, but with which he cannot raise immediately because he is too weak to raise to three, and too strong to raise to two.

Thus, with a hand worth 10-12 points in support of opener's suit, responder must temporize with a bid in a new suit before raising opener's suit.

Examples:

(a)   ♠ x x x   ♡ x   ◊ A x x x x   ♣ J x x x

Responder should raise a 1♠ opening to 2♠.

(b)   ♠ x x x x   ♡ K x x x   ◊ A x x   ♣ J x

Facing a 1♡ opening, responder should raise to 2♡. There

is no reason for responder to introduce his four-card spade suit when he has four-card support for his partner's major.

(c)   ♠ x x x   ♡ K x x   ◊ Q x x   ♣ Q x x x

Opposite a 1♠ opening, responder has neither four-card spade support nor shortness in any suit. He should thus respond 1 NT.

(d)   ♠ A J x   ♡ x x   ◊ K Q x x x   ♣ K x x

Worth a raise of an opening bid of 1◊ to 3◊. However, if the opening bid is 1♠, responder should bid 2◊, since he does not have four-card support for spades.

(e)   ♠ A J x x   ♡ x x   ◊ K Q x x   ♣ K x x

Worth a raise of an opening 1♠ bid to 3♠.

(f)   ♠ A J x x   ♡ x x   ◊ K Q x x   ♣ x x x

Too weak for a raise of 1♠ to 3♠ and too strong for a raise to 2♠, responder must temporize with a 2◊ bid over 1♠. He will show his true color at his next turn by making a minimum bid in spades

(g)   ♠ A J x x   ♡ x x   ◊ K Q x x x   ♣ K x

If opener has bid 1♠, responder should bid 2 diamonds before jumping in spades, to give a better picture of his hand for slam evaluation purposes. If opener had opened 1◊, responder should respond 1♠ with this hand, trying for the 10-trick spade game in preference to the 11-trick diamond game.

(h)   ♠ —   ♡ J x x x x   ◊ A K x x x x   ♣ A x

Facing a 1♡ opening bid, responder wants to play in 6♡ if opener has the Ace-King, Ace-Queen, or King-Queen of hearts. He should jump to 5♡ to ask opener to bid 6♡ with two of the top three heart honors.

(i)   ♠ Q x x x x   ♡ x   ◊ A x x x   ♣ x x x

Opposite a 1♠ opening, responder should jump to 4♠.

(j)   ♠ x   ♡ x   ◊ K J 10 x x x x x   ♣ x x x

Facing a 1◊ opening, responder should jump to 4◊. Responder may not expect to make 4◊, but hopes to prevent the opponents from finding their best contract.

RESPONDER'S NON-JUMP CHANGES OF SUIT

There are two general reasons why responder would bid a new suit in response to an opening bid of one. First, he may be looking for a better denomination in which to play the hand—either because he has a long suit of his own or because he is short in opener's suit.

Second, responder may be compelled to bid a new suit although he wants to play in opener's suit because he may have a hand that is the wrong strength for an immediate raise.

Generally responder should have four or more cards in the new suit in which he responds. No particular suit texture is required for a change of suit, although it is a wise policy to avoid bidding weak suits with very strong hands.

For a response at the two level in the suit that ranks just under opener's suit, responder should have at least five cards. Thus, in the auctions 1♠-2♡ or 1♡-2◊, responder promises a five- card or longer suit.

There are occasions on which responder will be forced to respond in a three-card suit rather than his long suit. These occasions occur chiefly when responder has 4-3-3-3 distribution and either has four cards in the suit just below opener's suit, or has four cards in opener's suit with 10-12 points and thus cannot make an immediate raise.

The strength required for a change of suit by responder varies with the level at which responder bids. The higher the level, the more points responder promises:

1-level response	6-18 points.
2-level non-jump response	10-18 points.
2-level or 3-level jump response	19 or more points.

Examples:

(a)   ♠ x x x   ♡ A x x x   ◇ A x x   ♣ K x x

Opposite a 1♡ opening, responder knows the hand should be played in hearts; yet he cannot raise to 2♡ because the single raise shows 6-9 points, and he has 11 high cards points. Nor can he jump to 3♡ because the jump raise promises 13-15 points. So responder should temporize with a response of 2♣. He will then bid 2♡ if opener rebids 2◇, raise a 2♡ rebid to 3♡, or bid 3♡ over a 2♠, 2 NT or 3♣ rebid. If the opening bid were 1♠, responder would still be compelled to respond 2♣ because he cannot respond 2♡ over 1♠ without promising a five-card suit.

(b)   ♠ x x x   ♡ A x x   ◇ A Q x x x   ♣ x x

After a 1◇ opening, a diamond raise by responder would not reflect his 11 point strength. He should respond 1♡, in-

tending to support diamonds on the next round. It may seem dangerous to respond in a three-card suit that is higher ranking than opener's suit, but the worst that can happen is that opener will insist on playing in hearts because he has good four-card support (for example, ♠ x x x ♡ K Q J x ◊ K J 10 x x ♣ A). In this case, the 4-3 fit could well provide the only makeable game.

IF RESPONDER HAS LENGTH IN 2 UNBID SUITS

If responder has two unbid suits that he wants to show, the order in which he bids them depends on their length and his overall strength.

If responder has two four-card suits	He should bid the cheaper one first (regardless of the strength of his hand, so long as he has the strength needed to show either). To bypass one suit in order to bid another, suggests that the first bid suit is at least five-cards long and is probably longer than the bypassed suit.
If responder has two five-card suits	He should, assuming he has the strength needed to go to the required level, bid the higher ranking suit first intending to re-bid twice in the lower suit to show at least 5-5 distribution.

If responder's suits are of unequal length, he should bid the longer suit first if he has sufficient strength to go to the level required.

If responder's longer suit ranks lower than his shorter suit and cannot be bid at the one level, he must have 10 points to show his longer suit at his first turn, and must have 13 or more points to show his longer suit first and then show his shorter suit later.

Examples (after an opening bid of 1 ◊):

(a) ♠ Q x x x   ♥ x x   ♦ K x x   ♣ A K x x

Responder should respond 1♠, the cheaper of his four-card suits, even though his clubs are stronger and he has enough high card strength to go to the two level. He should bid spades first in order not to give a distorted picture of his distribution.

(b) ♠ K Q x x x   ♥ A Q x x x   ♦ x   ♣ x x

Responder should bid 1♠ intending to rebid twice in hearts to show that he has at least five hearts. Since he bid spades first, he will thereby show also five or more spades.

(c) ♠ K x x x   ♥ x x   ♦ x x   ♣ A x x x x

Responder's clubs are longer than his spades, but he lacks the 10 points needed to allow him to go to the two level. The proper response is 1♠.

(d) ♠ K x x x   ♥ A x x x x   ♦ x   ♣ x x x

Responder should bid 1♡. Unless opener rebids in spades, responder will not be able to show his spade suit, for to do so at the 2 level after responding 1♡ would promise 13 points.

(e)   ♠ A x x x   ♡ x x x   ◇ x   ♣ A K x x x

Responder should bid 2♣ intending to show his four-card spade suit later. Bidding the suits in this order shows that his clubs are longer than his spades and that he has at least 13 points.

RESPONDER'S SINGLE JUMP SHIFT

With hands worth 19 or more points, responder may jump in a new suit. This response is forcing to game and strongly invites slam.

Examples (Opposite a 1♠ opening bid):

(a)   ♠ K J x x   ♡ x   ◇ x x   ♣ A K Q J x x

(b)   ♠ x x   ♡ A K Q x   ◇ x   ♣ A K Q x x x

(c)   ♠ K x   ♡ K Q x   ◇ A J x   ♣ K Q x x x

Responder should bid 3♣ on hands (a), (b), and (c). Hand (a) is the minimum with which a jump shift should be made; the good trump support and the solid six-card suit justify a slam invitation. Responder intends to support spades at his next turn and leave further aggressive action to opener.

(d)   ♠ A x x   ♡ A Q x x   ◇ A J x   ♣ A x x

Although it has the required 19 points, this hand is not suitable for a jump shift in a new suit because it does not have enough trick-taking potential to justify the issuance of a slam invitation. It is better to make the understated response of 2♣ in order to let opener describe his hand; If opener shows an unbalanced hand, the slam prospects become brighter.

RESPONDER'S DOUBLE JUMP
AND HIGHER JUMP SHIFTS

Double and triple jumps by responder in a new suit—e.g., from 1♡ to 4◇, or 1♡ to 4♠—are pre-emptive bids that show a very long suit but little high card strength and little tolerance for opener's suit.

Examples:

(e)   ♠ Q J 10 x x x x   ♡ x x   ◇ Q x x   ♣ x

Facing an opening bid of 1♣, 1◇, or 1♡, responder should bid 3♠.

(f)   ♠ x   ♡ x   ◇ K Q x x x x x   ♣ K x x

Responder should bid 5◇ over any opening bid.

NOTRUMP RESPONSES

Responses of 1, 2, 3, 6 and 7 NT are natural bids suggesting NT as a final contract. All of these responses except 1 NT are rather precise responses; they show narrowly defined high card point ranges, balanced distribution, and stoppers in all unbid suits. The response of 1 NT, by contrast, may be made with many distributions and no particular stoppers.

The point ranges are as follows:

1 NT   6-9 high card points in response to 1◇, 1♡, or 1♠.
       9-11 high card points in response to 1♣.

2 NT   13-15 high card points; forcing to game.

3 NT   16-18 high card points.

6 NT   21-23 high card points.

7 NT   24-28 high card points.

Examples in response to a 1♡ opening:

(a)   ♠ A J x x   ♡ x x x   ◇ K J x   ♣ K Q x

*Worth 14 points and has all of the unbid suits guarded.
2 NT response describes the hand perfectly.*

(b)   ♠ A x x   ♡ x x   ◇ A x x   ♣ K Q J x x

*Has 14 high card points, but is more oriented toward suit
play with its good five-card suit and its Aces. Has potential
for a slam in clubs. Responder should bid 2♣ in response to
the 1 ♡ opening. He is willing to settle for a NT contract
only after he has shown his clubs.*

(c)   ♠ A J x x   ♡ x x x   ◇ Q x   ♣ A Q J x

*Does not have a diamond stopper; responder should bid 1♠
rather than 2 NT.*

(d)   ♠ K Q x   ♡ Q x x   ◇ A Q x x   ♣ K J x

*Responder should jump to 3 NT, showing his 17 point bal-
anced hand.*

(e)   ♠ K x x   ♡ x x   ◇ K x x x   ♣ K x x x

Responder should respond 1 NT.

(f)   ♠ xx   ♡ xx   ◇ Axxxxx   ♣ Jxx

Too weak for responder to show his diamond suit, since he needs 10 points to bid at the two level. He should bid 1 NT.

Responses of 4 NT and 5 NT are artificial slam try responses. A 4 NT response is Blackwood; a 5 NT response is the Grand Slam Force.

OPENING SUIT BIDDER'S SECOND BID

The rules that folow assume that neither opponent has entered the auction.

Having opened with one of a suit, the second round of bidding is opener's first real opportunity to give precise information as to the strength and shape of his hand. His first rebid will usually clarify whether his hand is minimum (13-16 points), has extra strength (17-20 points), or is worth a game force (21 or more points).

Although many rebids show extra strength, the only rebid by opener that is forcing after a minimum response is the jump in a new suit.

SUMMARY OF STRENGTH
SHOWN BY OPENER'S SECOND BIDS

Opener's rebid options with hands of various strengths are as follows:

| Holding 13-16 points | Rebid of two of his own suit. |
| | Bid 1 NT. |

Raise responder's suit from one to two.

Raise responder's 2♡ response to a 1♠ opening to 3♡.

Holding 13-18 points

Bid in a new suit at a level that would permit responder to return to opener's first suit at the two level.

Holding 15-16 points

Raise a 1 NT response to a 1♣ opening to 2 NT.

Holding 15-18 points

Bid of 2 NT after a two level new suit response by responder. This bid is forcing to game since the partnership is known to have a minimum of 25 points.

Holding 16-19 points

Raise responder's two level new suit response of 2♣ or 2♢ to 3♣ or 3♢. This bid is forcing to game since the partnership is known to have at least 26 points.

Jump raise of responder's 2♡ response to a 1♠ opening to 4♡.

Holding 17-19 points

Jump bid of opener's own suit (showing at least a six-card suit of good texture).

Jump raise of responder's suit from one to three (showing at least four-card support).

Non-jump bid in a new suit at the three level.

Rebid his opening suit over a single raise by responder.

New suit over a single raise by responder.

Bid of 2 NT after a single raise by responder.

Raise a 1 NT response to a 1◊, 1♡, or 1♠ opening to 2 NT.

Raise a 1 NT response to a 1♠ opening to 3 NT.

Cue-bid in search of slam after a jump raise by responder of opener's suit.

Holding 19-20 points

Jump bid of game in opener's major suit.

Jump raise to four of responder's major suit.

Jump bid of 2 NT over a one-level suit response.

Jump bid of 3 NT over a two-level raise or new suit response.

Jump to 3 NT over a 1 NT response.

Non-jump bid in a new suit at the two level that does not permit responder to return to opener's first suit at the two level. This bid is known as a reverse. Reverses show very strong hands but are not absolutely forcing.

Holding 21 or more points	Jump in a new suit. This jump shift is the only bid by which opener can force responder to bid again.

SECOND BID BY OPENER AFTER A 1 NOTRUMP RESPONSE TO ORIGINAL SUIT BID OF 1

If the response has been 1 NT, showing 6-9 points (or 9-11 points over a 1♣ opening), opener should allow the hand to be played in NT if he has a balanced hand. A balanced distribution means 4-3-3-3 or 4-4-3-2 or 5-3-3-2.

Opener's proper second bids with a balanced hand after a response of 1 NT are as follows:

Opposite a NT response to an opening bid of 1◇, 1♡, or 1♠:

Holding 13-16 points	Opener should pass.
Holding 17-19 points	Opener should raise to 2 NT.
Holding 20-21 points	Opener should raise to 3 NT.

Opposite a NT response to an opening bid of 1♣:

Holding 13-14 points	Opener should pass.
Holding 15-16 points	Opener should raise to 2 NT.
Holding 17-21 points	Opener should jump to 3 NT.

With an unbalanced hand (i.e., a hand with a singleton, or void, or more than one doubleton), opener should retreat from 1 NT, either by rebidding his original suit (which to be rebiddable, must be at least five cards headed by the Queen and Jack) or by introducing a new suit.

If his original suit is only five cards long, opener should prefer to bid a second suit rather than rebidding his first suit, assuming he can bid the second suit at a level that is consistent with his strength.

Opener's proper second bids with an unbalanced hand after a 1 NT response are as follows.

Holding 13-18 points and no suit longer than five cards	Opener should bid at the two level in a new suit that ranks lower than his first suit. If he has no such biddable suit, he should rebid his first suit.
Holding 13-16 points with a six-card suit	Opener should bid two of his suit.
Holding 17-19 points with a (good) six-card suit	Opener should jump to three of his suit if it is a major or if he has a singleton. If his suit is a minor and he has no singleton, he should bid 2 NT. If his suit is not a good one (i.e., is headed by less than the K Q 10), he should bid a new suit or 2 NT.
Holding 19-20 points	Opener should jump to four of his suit if he has a good six-card or longer major. If he has no such suit and has no singleton, he should jump to 3 NT. if he has no such suit and has a singleton, he should bid at the two level in a suit that ranks higher than his first suit (a

reverse), or bid at the three level in a suit that ranks lower than his first suit (a jump shift).

Examples (after an opening of 1♡ and a response of 1 NT):

(a)   ♠ K x x   ♡ K Q x x x   ◊ A x x   ♣ J x

Opener should pass.

(b)   ♠ x x   ♡ A x x x x   ◊ A K x x   ♣ x x

Opener should bid 2 ◊ , showing his second suit.

(c)   ♠ Q x x x   ♡ A Q J x x   ◊ A x x   ♣ x

Opener cannot show his second suit, spades, without reversing, which would promise 19 points instead of the 15 he has. Opener should bid 2♡ .

(d)   ♠ K x x   ♡ A Q x x x   ◊ A K x x   ♣ x

Opener should bid 2◊ , showing his second suit. He hopes that responder will be able to bid again, so that opener can get in one more bid in order to show his extra strength; but if responder feels constrained to pass 2 ◊ , it is unlikely that a makeable game will have been missed.

(e)   ♠ A K Q x   ♡ A K 10 x x   ◊ Q x x   ♣ x

Strong enough for opener to try for game opposite the 6-9 points shown by responder. Opener should bid 2♠ —a reverse that promises 19-20 points and four spades, with at least five hearts.

(f)   ♠ Q x x x   ♡ A K 10 x x   ◊ J x   ♣ A K

*Opener should raise to 2 NT rather than introducing his
weakish spade suit.*

(g)   ♠ A x   ♡ K Q J x x x x   ◊ A x x   ♣ x

*Opener should jump to 3♡, promising a good six-card or
longer suit and 17-19 points.*

(h)   ♠ x   ♡ A K J x x   ◊ A x   ♣ K Q J x x

*A strong and very distributional hand. Opener should jump
to 3♣ over the 1 NT response to force responder to bid
again.*

SECOND BID BY OPENER IF RESPONDER HAS BID 2 NOTRUMP AFTER AN OPENING BID OF 1 IN A SUIT

If responder has made the game forcing response of 2 NT, promising
13-15 high card points, opener should calculate the total number of
points held by the partnership and either settle for game with 13-17
points, try for slam with 18-19 points, or insist on slam with 20 or
more points.

With any hand that contains a singleton or void, opener should
show a second suit if he has one, or rebid his suit if he has no second
suit.

If opener has a six-card or longer suit he should rebid it. If his
suit is a reasonably good one and he has slam interest, he should rebid it at the four level.

If opener has a hand with no singleton and no six-card suit, he
should be content to bid 3 NT if his hand is in the 13-17 point range.

The principal exception occurs when opener has bid 1♠ with

four spades and five hearts, or five spades and four hearts. In either of these cases, opener should rebid 3♡ over 2 NT, in part because if there is a 4-4 heart fit a 4♡ contract may be better than 3 NT, and in part because responder may have three-card spade support which he will show if he does not have four hearts. Thus, the 3♡ rebid will allow the partnership to locate either a 4-4 (or 5-4) heart fit or a 5-3 spade fit, which may fare better than 3 NT.

With any other hand that has two four-card suits or a five- card suit and a four-card suit but no singleton, opener should generally not show his second suit unless he holds 18 or more points and is interested in slam.

SECOND BID BY OPENER IF RESPONDER HAS BID 3 NOTRUMP AFTER AN OPENING BID OF 1 IN A SUIT

The response of 3 NT promises 16-18 high card points with stoppers in all of the unbid suits. To this total, opener should add his own points and calculate whether slam seems a reasonable possibility.

Any rebid by opener carries some slam implications.

With a six-card suit	Opener should rebid his suit.
With a second suit	Opener should bid it.
With a balanced hand worth 15-16 points	Opener should raise to 4 NT, asking responder to bid 6 NT with a maximum for his 3 NT response.
With 17-18 points	Opener should insist on a small slam, either by jumping to 6 NT or by bidding a new suit on the way to slam.

With 19-20 points   Opener should drive the hand to a small slam while inviting grand slam.

With 21-24 points   Opener should bid a grand slam.

SECOND BID BY OPENER
IF RESPONDER HAS BID 4 NOTRUMP OR 5 NOTRUMP
AFTER AN OPENING BID OF 1 IN A SUIT

A response of 4 NT is Blackwood. A response of 5 NT is the grand slam force. *See pages 204-206.*

SECOND BID BY OPENER IF RESPONDER
HAS RAISED OPENER'S BID OF 1 IN A SUIT TO 2

Opposite a single raise by responder, showing 6-9 points, opener should pass unless his hand is worth at least 17 points.

With 17-19 points, opener should either bid 2 NT with a balanced hand and stoppers in the unbid suits, or bid a new suit if he has one, or rebid his own suit. The bid of a new suit by opener after a raise forces responder to bid again.

Examples (if opener's 1♠ bid has been raised to 2♠):

(a)   ♠ A K x x x   ♡ x x   ◊ K Q x x   ♣ x x

Opener should pass.

(b)   ♠ A K x x x x   ♡ x   ◊ K Q x   ♣ K x x

Opener should rebid 3♠.

(c)   ♠ A K J x x   ♡ K x x   ◊ K J x x   ♣ x

Opener should rebid 3 ◊.

(d)   ♠ K J x x x   ♡ K Q x   ◊ A Q x   ♣ K x

Opener should rebid 2 NT. (Note that hand was too strong for a 1 NT opening with its 18 points plus a five- card suit).

With 20-21 points opener should see to it that game is reached. If he has a balanced hand with stopers in the unbid suits, he should jump to 3 NT. If he cannot bid 3 NT, he should bid game in his suit if his hand is very distributional, or bid a new suit in which he has length and strength.

With an even stronger two- or three-suited hand, opener should rebid his other suit or suits in an effort to explore for slam. For example, if opener has a hand such as

(e)   ♠ A K x x x   ♡ A x   ◊ A K x x x   ♣ x

slam might be reached even opposite so weak a responding hand as

(f)   ♠ Q x x x   ♡ x x   ◊ Q x x x x   ♣ x x

With hand (e) opposite hand (f), the auction might be:

(e)	*Opener*	*Responder*
	1♠	2♠
	3◊	4♠
	6◊	Pass

SECOND BID BY OPENER
IF RESPONDER HAS RAISED OPENER'S
OPENING BID OF 1 IN A MAJOR SUIT TO 3

Opposite a game forcing raise of his major suit to the three level, opener should assess whether or not his hand justifies a slam try.

If he has 17 or more points opposite responder's promised 13-15 points, he should try for slam. *See pp. 000-000.*

With a minimum hand of 13-16 points, opener should simply re-bid game in his suit.

SECOND BID BY OPENER
IF RESPONDER HAS RAISED OPENER'S
OPENING BID OF 1 IN A MINOR SUIT TO 3

After a game forcing raise of 1♣ to 3♣ or 1◊ to 3◊, opener must consider not only whether slam is a likelihood, but also whether the hand should be played in notrump rather than in the 11-trick minor suit game contract. Thus opener may rebid 3 NT if he has 13-15 points and stoppers in the unbid suits. Or he may bid a new suit, either in an effort to reach 3 NT with a hand in which he has one or more suits unstopped, or as a cue-bid trying for slam.

Examples (After a 1◊ opening and a 3◊ response):

(a)   ♠ K x   ♡ A x x   ◊ K Q x x x   ♣ J x x

Opener should bid 3 NT.

(b)   ♠ x x   ♡ A Q x   ◊ K Q x x x   ♣ K J x

With no spade stopper, opener should bid 3♡, hoping that responder has a spade stopper so that he can either bid 3 NT with both spades and clubs guarded, or bid 3♣ with spades, but not clubs, guarded.

(c)   ♠ x   ♡ A x x   ◊ A Q x x x x   ♣ A x x

Opener should bid 3♡ here also, but not with a view to passing 3 NT if responder makes that bid; here opener intends to make a further cue-bid of 4♣ to show his fine suit- oriented playing hand.

(d)   ♠ x   ♡ x x   ◊ A Q x x x x   ♣ K Q x x

Opener should simply bid 4◊, leaving any slam tries to responder.

SECOND BID BY OPENER IF RESPONDER HAS RAISED OPENER'S MAJOR SUIT OPENING BID OF 1 TO 4, OR HAS RAISED OPENER'S MINOR SUIT OPENING BID OF 1 TO 4 OR 5

Opposite a pre-emptive double or triple jump raise of opener's suit, which promises less than 10 high card points but shows very uneven distribution, opener should normally pass unless he has at least two aces and very good playing strength.

Examples (If opener's 1♠ bid has been raised to 4♠):

(a)   ♠ A K x x x   ♡ x   ◊ K Q x   ♣ K Q J x

Opener should pass.

(b)   ♠ A K x x x   ♡ A K x x x   ◊ K x x   ♣ —

Opening should try for slam by cue-bidding 5♣.

(c)   ♠ A K x x x x   ♡ K Q x x   ◇ A K   ♣ x

Opener should try for slam. Blackwood is the proper try.

If opener's 1 ◇ bid has been raised to 4 ◇ :

(d)   ♠ K Q   ♡ x x x   ◇ A Q x x   ♣ K x x x

Opener should pass.

(e)   ♠ A K x   ♡ x x   ◇ A Q x x   ♣ A x x x

Opener should continue to 5 ◇. If opener's 1 ◇ bid had been raised to 5 ◇, opener should pass.

SECOND BID BY OPENER IF RESPONDER HAS RAISED OPENER'S MAJOR SUIT OPENING BID OF 1 TO 5

Responder's jump from 1♡ to 5♡ or from 1♠ to 5♠ is a slam try asking opener to bid six of his suit if he has good trumps. Opener should bid the small slam if he has either the Ace-King, the King-Queen, or the Ace-Queen of his suit. Otherwise he should pass.

SECOND BID BY OPENER IF RESPONDER HAS RAISED OPENER'S SUIT OPENING BID OF 1 TO 6

When responder has blasted into slam in this fashion, opener should pass.

SECOND BID BY OPENER AFTER
NON-JUMP CHANGE OF SUIT BY RESPONDER

After a response in a new suit, the range of which is quite wide (8 to 18 points for a 1-level response, 10 to 18 points for a 2-level response), opener has four types of rebids available: the raise, the bid of a new suit, the rebid of his own suit, and the notrump rebid.

(1) In order to make a non-jump raise of responder's suit, opener should have either four-card support, or three cards headed by a high honor and a doubleton in a side suit. A jump raise of responder's suit (showing greater strength) promises four trumps, except when opener has opened with 1♠ and the response has been 2♡. In that auction the 2♡ bid promises at least five hearts, and opener is allowed to jump to 4♡ with as few as three hearts.

(2) Opener may bid a new suit if he has one that he can show consistently with the strength of his hand. He is not allowed to bid his new suit at the three level, even as a non-jump, unless he has at least 17 points: He is not allowed to bid his second suit at the two level if it is higher in rank than his first suit (a "reverse"), unless he has 19 or 20 points.

(3) Opener may rebid his original suit if he has an unbalanced one-suited hand and a rebiddable suit.

(4) Opener may rebid in notrump if (a) he has the unbid suits guarded in a balanced hand, (b) he does not have a second suit that he has enough strength to bid, and (c) his hand is not suitable for a raise of responder's suit. In order for opener to rebid in NT after responder's response at the two-level, opener must have 15 to 18 high card points.

If opener takes any of the above actions over a one-level response without jumping he does not promise great strength. However, if a two-over-one response of 2♣ or 2♦ is raised to the three level, opener promises at least 16 points.

A jump raise of responder's suit or a jump rebid in opener's suit promises 17-19 points; a jump in NT promises at least 19 points. These jumps strongly encourage responder to bid again.

If responder has responded in a new suit at the two-level, any reverse or any other bid by opener of 2 NT or higher forces the partnership to game, since the partnership is known to have a minimum of 25 or 26 points.

A jump shift forces responder to bid again, even if he has promised no more than 6 to 9 points.

Examples:

(a)   ♠ Q x x   ♡ A Q x x x   ◇ J x   ♣ A x x

Opener would open 1♡ and over a 1♠ response, would raise to 2♠. Over a 2♣ or 2◇ response, however, he would bid 2♡, his hand being too weak to rebid 2 NT over the 2◇ response or to raise the 2♣ response to 3♣.

(b)   ♠ J x   ♡ Q x x   ◇ A Q x x x   ♣ A x x

Opener would open 1◇ and raise a 1♡ response to 2♡, or bid 1 NT over a 1♠ response.

(c)   ♠ J x   ♡ A J x x x   ◇ K Q J x   ♣ K x

After opening 1♡, opener would bid 2◇ after a 1♠, 1 NT or 2♣ response, or would raise a 2◇ response to 3◇.

(d)   ♠ K Q x x   ♡ A x x   ◇ A Q x x x   ♣ x

After opening with 1◇, opener would bid 1♠ after a 1♡ response; it is not appropriate to raise responder's heart suit on three-card support when opener has a second suit of his own that he can bid. If the response to the 1◇ opening were 2♣, opener would bid 2◊; if the response to 1◊ were 1♠, opener would jump raise to 3♠.

(e)   ♠ A x x   ♡ A K J x x x   ◊ K x x   ♣ x

Opener should open 1♡ and bid 3♡ over any non-jump response.

(f)   ♠ x   ♡ A K Q x x   ◊ x   ♣ K Q J x x x

Opener should open 1♣ and bid 2♡ over a 1◊ or 1♠ response. The jump to 2♡ over a 1◊ response is forcing. The "reverse" rebid of 2 ♡ after a 1♠ response is not forcing, but it promises 19-20 points. Since responder promises 6-9 points, he rarely passes the reverse.

(g)   North   East   South   West
         1♣   Pass   1♡   2◊
         2♠

The 2♠ bid by opener is not a reverse, even though responder cannot support clubs at the two level because if West had not intervened with 2◊, opener would have been able to rebid 1♠, thus allowing responder to bid clubs at the two level. Thus, the 2♠ bid here does not show extra strength.

SECOND BID BY OPENER AFTER RESPONDER HAS MADE A SINGLE JUMP IN A NEW SUIT AFTER AN OPENING SUIT BID OF 1

After a jump shift by responder, showing 19 or more points, opener should bid his hand as naturally as possible. He may raise responder's suit with three or more cards, or with a doubleton if it is headed by the Ace, King, or Queen.

He may bid a second suit if it is a reasonable suit (Q J x x or better).

He may rebid his original suit if it contains at least five cards and has good texture (K Q x x x or better) and if he has no good second suit to show.

If opener's hand is unsuitable for any of the above actions he can bid notrump if he has stoppers in the unbid suits.

If opener's hand is suitable for more than one of the above actions, he should make the rebid that he thinks will give responder the most valuable information.

Examples:

(a)   ♠ A K x x   ♡ x x   ◊ A J x x x   ♣ x x

After opening with 1 ◊ and receiving a 3 ♣ response, opener should bid 3 ♠, showing his second suit.

(b)   ♠ J x x x   ♡ x x   ◊ A K J x x   ♣ A x

After opener has bid 1 ◊ and received a 2 ♡ response, his proper bid is 3 ◊. His spade suit is too weak to show, and his diamond suit is quite strong.

(c)   ♠ K x   ♡ A x   ◊ K J x x x   ♣ Q x x x

After a 1 ◊ opening and a 2 ♠ response, opener's diamond suit is not rebiddable in these circumstances and his club suit is not biddable; thus opener should raise opener's suit with K x.

(d)   ♠ K Q x   ♡ A x x x x   ◊ K J x   ♣ J x

After a 1 ♡ opening and a 3 ♣ response, opener should bid 3 NT.

(e)   ♠ A x x x   ♡ Q x   ◊ A K Q x x x   ♣ x

Having opened with 1◊ and received a 2♡ response, open-er could properly show either his four-card spade suit or his long diamonds. Having a high honor in responder's suit, it is far more likely that the hand should play in hearts, even if responder happens also to have four spades; thus opener should prefer to rebid his long solid diamonds rather than introducing spades, as the knowledge that opener has a good diamond suit is likely to be more useful to responder.

(f)   ♠ A x x x   ♡ Q x x   ◊ A K Q x x x   ♣ —

After opening with 1◊ and hearing a 2♡ response, opener should, in this instance, choose to raise responder's hearts, because that bid establishes the trump suit, after which opener will be in a position to use the grand slam force, ask-ing responder to bid 7♡ if he has the Ace and King of hearts.

SECOND BID BY OPENER AFTER RESPONDER HAS MADE A PRE-EMPTIVE DOUBLE JUMP, OR A TRIPLE JUMP, OR A HIGHER JUMP IN A NEW SUIT AFTER AN OPENING SUIT BID OF 1

After a pre-emptive double or triple jump shift by responder, opener should pass unless he has a hand that is rich in Aces and Kings and has a good fit for responder's suit. If he has such a special hand he may consider raising responder's suit. He should make no further attempt to play the hand in his own suit.

Examples:

(a)   ♠ xx   ♡ KQxx   ◊ AKJxx   ♣ xx

Having opened 1◊, if responder jumps to 3♣, opener should pass. However, if responder jumps to 3♡, opener should raise to 4♡. Whether or not 4♡ can be made, it seems likely that the opponents can make something in spades or clubs.

(b)   ♠ Ax   ♡ Axx   ◊ AKxxxx   ♣ Qx

After a 1◊ opening and a 5♣ response, opener should chance a raise to 6♣.

SECOND BID BY OPENER
AFTER RESPONDER HAS PASSED AND
THE OPPONENTS HAVE KEPT THE BIDDING OPEN

If responder has passed but opener has another chance to bid because the opponents have overcalled or doubled, any action by opener—whether bidding a new suit, rebidding his own suit, bidding NT, doubling or redoubling—shows a considerably better than minimum hand. Opener does not need to jump in this type of competitive auction to show a good hand, and should do so only on those very rare hands with which he can make his bid in his own hand, since his partner has shown 0-5 points.

REPLIES BY RESPONDER TO OPENER'S SECOND BID

By the time opener has bid and rebid over responder's initial response, responder's goal has been somewhat clarified. He can usually, although not always, evaluate his hand in terms of whether he wants to force to game while inviting slam, bid a game while discouraging slam exploration, invite a game, accept a game invitation, reject a game invitation, or make a non-committal or waiting rebid.

Responder should bear in mind that any bid by him in a new suit forces opener to bid again unless opener has rebid 1 NT. If opener has rebid 1 NT, a rebid by responder in a new suit that ranks lower than his first suit is not forcing; however, a rebid by responder in a new suit that ranks higher than his first suit is a reverse and forces opener to continue bidding until game is reached.

Any reverse by responder promises 13 or more points and is forcing to game. In addition, any jump rebid by responder is forcing to game.

REPLIES BY RESPONDER IF OPENER HAS RAISED AN INITIAL RESPONSE OF 1 NOTRUMP

If opener has raised 1 NT to 2 NT

If the opening bid was 1 ◊ , 1 ♡ , or 1 ♠ , responder should bid 3 NT if he has 9 points or 8 points with a good five-card suit. He should pass with 6 or 7 points or with a poor 8. If the opening bid was 1 ♣ , responder should bid 3 NT with 10 or 11 points; with 9 points, or a poor 10 points, he should pass.

If opener has raised 1 NT to 3 NT	Responder should pass.

REPLIES BY RESPONDER IF OPENER HAS REBID HIS SUIT OVER RESPONDER'S INITIAL RESPONSE OF 1 NOTRUMP

If opener has rebid 2 of his suit over 1 NT	Responder should pass. Game is hardly likely.
If opener has rebid 3 of his suit over 1 NT	Responder should bid game with 8-10 points, and pass with less.

If these 8-10 points are largely in Queens and Jacks and he has a singleton or doubleton in opener's suit and guards in the other suits, his rebid should be 3 NT.

If responder has three cards in opener's suit and if his 8-10 points are mostly in Aces and Kings, he should raise opener's suit to game.

If opener has rebid game in his suit over 1 NT	Responder should pass.

Examples—If opener has opened 1♡ *and rebid* 3♡ *over responder's 1 NT response:*

(a)   ♠ Q x x   ♡ x x   ◊ Q x x x   ♣ Q x x x

Responder should pass.

(b)   ♠ A x x   ♡ 10 x   ◊ K J x   ♣ x x x x x

Responder should raise to 4♡ .

(c)   ♠ K J x   ♡ x x   ◊ Q J x   ♣ Q x x x x

Responder should bid 3 NT.

A typical hand for opener might be:

(d)   ♠ x x   ♡ A K J x x x   ◊ A x   ♣ K x x

REPLIES BY RESPONDER IF OPENER HAS MADE A NON-JUMP BID IN A NEW SUIT OVER RESPONDER'S INITIAL RESPONSE OF 1 NOTRUMP

When opener has bid two suits and responder has responded 1 NT to the first bid, responder's responsibility is to tell opener which suit responder prefers.

If responder has equal length in opener's two suits, he should prefer the suit that opener bid first.

If responder's length in opener's two suits is unequal, he will prefer the suit in which he has the greater length.

If responder prefers opener's first suit, he simply bids it. If opener has not reversed and responder prefers opener's second suit, he either passes if he has 6-8 points, or raises the second suit to the 3 level if he has 9-10 points and a good fit for the second suit.

In the special case in which responder has 10 points, most of which are in the two unbid suits, and has two cards in opener's first suit and three in the second suit, responder may bid 2 NT over opener's second bid.

If opener has reversed, showing 19-20 points, responder should make an effort to bid again even with a minimum. He may bid whichever of opener's suits he prefers, or bid 2 NT, or rebid a good five-card suit.

Examples—If the bidding has begun:

Opener	Responder
1♠	1 NT
2◊	

(a)   ♠J x   ♡ Q x x x   ◊ J x   ♣ Q x x x x

While responder's length in opener's two suits is equal, opener is likely to have greater length in his first suit than in his second. Responder should thus bid 2♠.

(b)   ♠ A K   ♡ x x x x   ◊ x x x   ♣ x x x x

Opener should pass 2◊; although he has far greater high card strength in opener's first suit, he is asked to take a preference based on length, not strength.

(c)   ♠ x   ♡ A x x x   ◊ A x x x x   ♣ x x x

Responder has an excellent fit for diamonds and a good hand for his 1 NT response. He should raise to 3◊.

(d)   ♠ x x   ♡ K J 10 x   ◊ J x x   ♣ A J x x

Responder should bid 2 NT.

REPLIES BY REPONDER IF OPENER
HAS JUMPED IN A NEW SUIT OVER
RESPONDER'S INITIAL RESPONSE OF 1 NOTRUMP

After a jump bid by opener in a new suit, responder is asked to take a preference between opener's two suits based on his length in each. Even with the barest minimum responder cannot pass, since the jump shift is forcing to game. Responder must show his preference.

After a jump shift at the three level, responder should be wary of bypassing 3 NT. He may cue-bid an Ace or King in an effort to reach 3 NT or on the way to a slam invitational raise.

Examples—If the bidding has begun:
Opener	Responder
1♡	1 NT
3♣	

(a)   ♠ Q x x   ♡ x x x   ◇ K J x x   ♣ x x x

Responder should bid 3♡; he prefers opener's first bid suit since he has equal length in the two suits.

(b)   ♠ Q x x   ♡ x x   ◇ K J x x x   ♣ x x x

Although responder has greater length in opener's second suit (clubs), he should not raise clubs but should bid 3 NT since his hand offers little reason to believe there is a slam lurking in one of opener's suits.

(c)   ♠ K Q x   ♡ x x   ◇ J x x x   ♣ x x x x

Responder prefers clubs and should cue-bid 3♠. Responder hopes to hear opener bid 3 NT, which responder will pass.

(d)   ♠ A x x   ♡ x x   ◇ x x x x   ♣ A x x x

Responder prefers clubs and should cue-bid 3♠. Responder intends to raise clubs later, and cue-bids spades first to show that Ace.

REPLIES BY RESPONDER
IF OPENER HAS REBID HIS SUIT AFTER
RESPONDER'S INITIAL RAISE FROM 1 TO 2

If opener has opened in a major and has rebid 3 of his suit

Responder should bid game in the agreed suit if he has 8 or 9 points. Otherwise he should pass.

If opener has opened in a minor suit and has rebid 3 of his suit

If responder has 8 or 9 points: he should bid 3 NT if he has both major suits stopped; if one major suit is unguarded, he should bid 3 of the other major; if both are unguarded, he should bid four of the agreed suit. If responder has 6 or 7 points, he should pass.

If opener has rebid game in his suit

Responder should pass.

If opener has rebid 5 of his major suit

Responder should bid six of the agreed trump suit if he holds one of the top three honors in the suit. Opener undoubtedly has an unusual hand such as:

♠ Q x x x x x x   ♡ A K Q   ◇ A K x   ♣ —

If opener has rebid 6 of his suit	Responder should pass.

REPLIES BY RESPONDER IF OPENER HAS REBID IN NOTRUMP AFTER RESPONDER'S INITIAL RAISE OF OPENER'S SUIT FROM 1 TO 2

If opener has rebid 2 NT over the raise	If responder has 8 or 9 points: he should bid 3 NT if his hand is balanced or if the suit is a minor; if the suit is a major and his hand is unbalanced, he should bid four of the major.
	If responder has 6 or 7 points: he should pass 2 NT if his hand is balanced, or bid three of the agreed suit if his hand is unbalanced.
If opener has rebid 3 NT over the raise	Responder should bid four of opener's suit if it is a major and responder holds four-card support and a side singleton or void.
	Otherwise responder should pass.

Examples—If the auction has begun:

Opener	Responder
1♠	2♠
2 NT	

(a)   ♠ Q x x   ♡ x x x   ◊ Q x x   ♣ K x x x

Responder should pass.

(b)   ♠ Q x x x   ♡ x   ◊ K x x x x   ♣ x x x

Responder should return to 3♠.

(c)   ♠ J x x   ♡ x x   ◊ K Q x x   ♣ K x x x

Responder should raise to 3 NT.

(d)   ♠ J x x x   ♡ A x x x   ◊ x   ♣ Q x x x

Responder should jump to 4♠.

REPLIES BY RESPONDER IF OPENER HAS REBID IN A NEW SUIT AFTER RESPONDER'S RAISE OF OPENER'S FIRST SUIT FROM 1 TO 2

Opener's rebid of a new suit after responder has raised to the two level is a game invitation. Since trumps have been agreed upon, the new suit bid is, as a practical matter, forcing for one round.

If responder has 6-7 points or a poor 8, he should reject the invitation by returning to three of opener's first suit.

With 8-9 points, he should accept the invitation by jumping to game in opener's first suit, raising opener's second suit, or bidding NT if he has the unbid suits stopped.

Examples—If the auction has begun:

Opener	Responder
1♡	2♡
3♣	

(a)   ♠ Q x x   ♡ K x x   ◊ Q x x   ♣ J x x x

Responder should simply return to 3♡.

(b)   ♠ xxx   ♡ Kxxx   ◇ x   ♣ AJxxx

Responder should jump to 4♡ .

(c)   ♠ xxx   ♡ Kxx   ◇ xx   ♣ Axxxx

Responder should raise to 4♣ .

(d)   ♠ Kxx   ♡ Qxx   ◇ KJxxx   ♣ xx

Responder should bid 3 NT.

REPLIES BY RESPONDER
IF OPENER HAS REBID HIS SUIT AFTER
RESPONDER'S INITIAL JUMP RESPONSE OF 2 NOTRUMP

If opener has rebid 3 of his suit over a 2 NT response, it shows a six-card suit or a very good five-card suit and a singleton somewhere. Responder should content himself with a game bid unless his hand is rich in Aces and Kings and he has a high honor in opener's suit. In the latter case, responder should cue-bid to issue a mild slam invitation.

Examples—If the auction has begun:

Opener	Responder
1♡	2 NT
3♡	

(a)   ♠ KJ10x   ♡ Jx   ◇ AJ10   ♣ KJ10x

Responder should rebid 3 NT. This hand rates to be most valuable in a NT contract with the lead coming up to its ten-aces. The hand does not offer good prospects for slam.

(b)   ♠ K J 10 x   ♡ K x   ◊ A x x   ♣ Q x x x

*Responder should raise to 4♡ for lack of good slam pros-
pects. Unlike hand (a), hand (b) rates to play better in
opener's suit.*

(c)   ♠ A J x   ♡ K x   ◊ A x x x   ♣ K x x x

*An excellent hand for a slam invitation. Responder should
cue-bid 3♠.*

If opener has rebid game in his suit over 2 NT, it shows a good six-
card suit and is a mild slam invitation. Responder should pass with
hands (a) or (b) above; he should cue-bid 4♠ with hand (c).

REPLIES BY RESPONDER
IF OPENER HAS REBID IN NOTRUMP AFTER
RESPONDER'S INITIAL JUMP RESPONSE OF 2 NOTRUMP

If opener has rebid 3 NT over responder's jump to 2 NT, responder
should pass.
    If opener has raised 2 NT to 4 NT, responder should bid 6 NT
with 15 points or with a very good 14; with less, he should pass.

REPLIES BY RESPONDER
IF OPENER HAS REBID IN A NEW SUIT AFTER
RESPONDER'S INITIAL JUMP RESPONSE OF 2 NOTRUMP

If opener has rebid 3 of a new suit over 2 NT, and responder has
three cards in opener's first suit, he should return to that suit unless
opener has bid both majors. If responder has four cards in the second
major, he should raise that suit.

Example:

(a)   *Opener   Responder*
     1♠   2 NT
     3♡

Responder should raise to 4♡ if he has four hearts, even if he also has three-card spade support. This is because opener may have four spades and four hearts, or four spades and five hearts. Even if opener has five spades and four hearts, the 4-4 fit may produce one trick more than the 5-3 fit.

If responder has a doubleton in opener's first suit and fewer than four cards in his second suit, he should rebid 3 NT.

If responder has a doubleton in opener's first suit and holds four cards in opener's second suit, he should rebid 3 NT only if he has a concentration of his points in the unbid suits; otherwise, he should raise opener's second suit.

Examples—If the auction has begun:
   Opener   Responder
     1♡   2 NT
     3◇

(b)   ♠ K Q x   ♡ K x x   ◇ A x x x   ♣ Q x x

Responder should show that he has three hearts by bidding 3♡.

(c)   ♠ K J x x   ♡ x x   ◇ K x x   ♣ A K x x

Responder should rebid 3 NT.

(d)   ♠ A x x   ♡ x x   ◊ A Q x x   ♣ K x x x

Responder should cue-bid 3♠ on the way to raising diamonds.

REPLIES BY RESPONDER OVER VARIOUS REBIDS BY OPENER IF RESPONDER'S FIRST BID WAS A JUMP RAISE OF OPENER'S SUIT

If opener has rebid game in the suit

Responder should pass.

If opener has bid 3 NT over the jump raise

If responder has a singleton, and the suit is a major, he should bid four of the suit. Otherwise he should pass.

If opener has bid a new suit after a jump raise of his major suit

Any new suit bid by opener after a jump major suit raise by responder is a cue-bid in search of slam. Responder should cooperate if he has better than a minimum for his jump raise.

If opener has bid a new suit after a jump raise of his minor suit

A new suit bid by opener after a jump raise by responder *in a minor suit* is ambiguous: It may show a stopper in the new suit, searching for 3 NT. Or it may be a cue-bid in search of slam. Responder should normally bid 3 NT if he has the unbid suits guarded. If responder lacks the needed stoppers *or* if his hand is rich in Aces and Kings, he should cue-bid.

Examples:

(a)   ♠ Q J x x   ♡ x   ◊ A K x x   ♣ Q x x x

With this hand, responder has raised opener's 1♠ opening to 3♠. If opener rebids 4♠, responder should pass; if opener rebids 3 NT, responder should bid 4♠; if opener cue-bids 4♣, responder should cue-bid 4◊.

(b)   ♠ A K x   ♡ x x   ◊ K Q x x x   ♣ x x x

With this hand, responder has raised a 1◊ opening to 3◊. If opener rebids 3♡, responder should bid 3♠. If, instead, opener had:

(c)   ♠ A J x   ♡ x x   ◊ K J x x   ♣ K J x x

Responder should bid 3 NT over 3♡.

REPLIES BY RESPONDER
IF OPENER'S SECOND BID WAS 1 NOTRUMP

If opener's second bid was 1 NT, responder knows that opener has a hand worth exactly 13-15 points. Responder should:

>Sign off with 6-10 points
>
>Try for game with 11-12 points
>
>Force to game with 13-17 points
>
>Try for slam with 18-19 points

The only bid available to responder that is unambiguously a game invitation is the raise to 2 NT.

Any jump rebid by responder shows at least 13 points and is forcing to game. Any reverse by responder, i.e., a bid in a suit that ranks higher than the first suit he has bid, also shows at least 13 points and is forcing to game.

SUMMARY OF REPLIES BY RESPONDER IF OPENER'S SECOND BID WAS 1 NOTRUMP

If Responder Has a Strong Hand (13-19 points):

And has no singleton and no six-card suit	Responder may jump to 3 NT with 13-17 points; with 18-19 points, he should reverse or jump.
And has four-card support for opener's suit	He may jump to three of opener's suit.
And has a six-card suit of his own	He may jump to three of his suit.
And has a second suit	He may jump to three of that suit if it ranks lower than his first suit or bid it without jumping if it ranks higher than his first suit; in either of these events, he promises at least five cards in his first suit and at least four cards in his second suit.

If Responder Has Intermediate Strength (11-12 points):

And has a hand without four cards in opener's suit, without a six-card suit, and without a singleton

Responder should bid 2 NT.

And has four cards in opener's suit

Responder should bid two of opener's suit, hoping that opener will bid again.

And his own suit is six cards long and he has no second suit

Responder should normally rebid two of his suit. However, if his suit is solid or semi-solid and he has no singleton, he should bid 2 NT.

And his first suit is six cards long and he has a second suit of four cards

Responder should bid his second suit if it ranks below his first suit. If it ranks higher than his first suit, he should bid two of his first suit.

And his first suit is five or more cards long, and he has a second suit that contains more than four cards

Responder should bid two of his second suit.

And his first suit is five cards long, and he has a second suit that is four cards long, and has three cards in opener's suit

Responder should bid two of his second suit if it ranks lower than his first suit. If it ranks higher than his first suit, he should bid two of opener's suit.

And his first suit is five cards long and he has a second suit that is four cards long and has a singleton in opener's suit	Responder should bid two of his second suit if it ranks lower than his first suit. If it ranks higher than his first suit, he should pass 1 NT if his points consist mostly of Queens and Jacks; he should rebid his first suit if it has good texture and his points are mostly in Aces and Kings.
And he has 4-4-4-1 distribution with a singleton in opener's suit	If the opening bid has been 1 ◇ or 1 ♡, responder should bid 2♣ over opener's 1 NT rebid. If the opening bid has been 1♣ and responder has bid 1◇, he should pass opener's 1 NT rebid.

If Responder Has a Minimum Responding Hand (6-10 points):

And he has a hand without four cards in opener's suit, without a six-card suit, and without a singleton	Responder should pass 1 NT.
And he has four cards in opener's suit	Responder should bid two of opener's suit.
And his own suit is six cards long and he has no second suit that is more than four cards long	Responder should bid two of his suit, regardless of whether or not he has a side four-card suit.

And he has a second suit that contains more than four cards	Responder should bid two of his second suit if it ranks lower than his first suit. If it ranks higher than his first suit, he should rebid his first suit.
And his first suit is five cards long, and he has a second suit that is four cards long, and he has three cards in opener's suit	Responder should bid two of opener's suit.
And his first suit is five cards long, and he has a second suit that is four cards long, and he has a singleton in opener's suit	Responder should pass 1 NT.
And he has 4-4-4-1 distribution with a singleton in opener's suit	Responder should pass 1 NT.

Examples—If the auction has begun:

Opener	Responder
1 ◇	1 ♠
1 NT	

(a)   ♠ K Q x x   ♡ Q x   ◇ A x x x   ♣ x x x

Responder should bid 2 NT.

(b)   ♠ A x x x   ♡ x   ◇ K x x x   ♣ x x x x

Responder should bid 2 ◇ .

(c)   ♠ K J x x   ♡ x x   ◊ x   ♣ Q x x x x x

Responder should bid 2♣.

(d)   ♠ K x x x x   ♡ x x   ◊ Q x x x   ♣ x

Responder should bid 2♠.

After the auction has begun:
Opener   Responder
   1◊   1♡
   1 NT

(e)   ♠ A x x x   ♡ A K x x x   ◊ x   ♣ Q x x

*Responder should rebid 2♠, a reverse that promises 13
points and is forcing to game. He makes the rebid in spades
not because he expects opener to have a spade suit (opener
has denied having four spades by failing to bid 1♠ and
instead rebidding 1 NT); but because the 2♠ bid describes
both his strength and his distribution.*

(f)   ♠ A x x x   ♡ Q x x x x   ◊ Q x x   ♣ x

*Responder lacks the strength to show his distribution by bid-
ding 2♠. He returns to two of opener's suit—2◊—because
he has a singleton. He would make the same 2◊ rebid with
four-card diamond support or with two more points.*

(g)   ♠ x x x x   ♡ K x x x x   ◊ x x   ♣ A x

*Responder lacks the strength to show his distribution by bid-
ding 2♠. Having no singleton, he passes 1 NT. He would
also pass if he had one more club and one less diamond.*

(h)   ♠ A x x   ♡ K Q 10 9 x x   ◊ x x   ♣ x x

Responder should raise to 2 NT.

(i)   ♠ A x x   ♡ Q J x x x x   ◊ K x   ♣ x x

Responder should rebid 2 ♡ .

REPLIES BY RESPONDER
IF OPENER HAS REBID 2 NOTRUMP OVER
RESPONDER'S INITIAL BID OF 2 IN A NEW SUIT

If opener has rebid 2 NT over responder's 2-level new suit response, opener promises 15-18 points.

Since responder's initial two-over-one response promised at least 10 points, opener's rebid forces the partnership to game, for the partnership has at the very least 25 points. With 15-17 points, responder should try for a slam.

If responder has four cards in opener's suit or has three cards headed by an honor and has a side doubleton

He should bid three of opener's suit.

If responder has a second suit of his own

He should bid three of that suit.

If responder has a six-card suit

He should rebid it.

If responder has none of the above distributions

He should raise in NT to 3 NT with 10-14 points; to 4 NT with 15-17 high card points; or to 6 NT with 18 high card points.

Examples—If the auction has started:

Opener	Responder
1♠	2♣
2 NT	

(a)   ♠ KQxx   ♡ xx   ◇ xx   ♣ AJxxx

Responder should bid 3♠. Opener will allow for the possibilities that responder has only three spades or that he has only 11-12 points and thus could not make an immediate forcing jump to 3♠.

(b)   ♠ xxx   ♡ KJxx   ◇ Qx   ♣ AQxx

Responder should bid 3 NT despite his three-card spade support since his hand is balanced.

(c)   ♠ xx   ♡ Kx   ◇ Axx   ♣ AQJxxx

Responder should bid 3♣. Responder can envision a slam if opener has a suitable hand.

(d)   ♠ xx   ♡ AKxx   ◇ x   ♣ AQxxxx

Responder should bid 3♡.

REPLIES BY RESPONDER
IF OPENER'S SECOND BID WAS A JUMP TO 2 NOTRUMP
OVER RESPONDER'S FIRST BID OF ONE IN A SUIT

If opener has jumped to 2 NT over responder's 1-level suit response, that bid promises 19-21 high card points.

With 6 points, responder should pass. Any rebid commits the partnership to game.

With 7-11 points, he should bid toward game.

With 12-13 points, he should try for slam.

With 14-15 points, he should force to a small slam.

If responder has more than 6 points, he should take the following actions:

With a six-card or longer suit	Responder should rebid three of his suit if it is a major and he has 7-11 points. If it is a major and he has 12-13 points, he should jump to four of his suit; this jump is a mild slam try. If his suit is a minor, he should bid 3 NT with 7-11 points, or bid three of his suit with 12-13 points. The rebid of the minor suit at the three level is a mild slam try.
With four cards in opener's suit	Responder should bid three of opener's suit.
With a five-card suit and a second suit	Responder should bid his second suit if he has 12 or more points, or if he has a singleton in an unbid suit. Otherwise, he should bid 3 NT.
With any other distribution	Responder should bid in NT: 3 NT with 7-11 points; 4 NT with 12-13 points; 6 NT with 14-15 points; 5 NT with 16-17 points; or 7 NT with 18-21 points.

Examples—If the auction has begun:

Opener	Responder
1◊	1♡
2NT	

(a)   ♠ xx   ♡ KJxx   ◊ xxxx   ♣ Axx

Responder should bid 3 NT.

(b)   ♠ KQxx   ♡ AKxxx   ◊ xx   ♣ xx

Responder should bid 3♠.

(c)   ♠ xxx   ♡ AQxxx   ◊ KQxx   ♣ x

Responder should bid 3◊.

(d)   ♠ xx   ♡ KQxxxx   ◊ xx   ♣ Axx

Responder should bid 4♡.

(e)   ♠ Ax   ♡ Qxxxxx   ◊ xx   ♣ xxx

Responder should bid 3♡.

REPLIES BY RESPONDER IF OPENER'S SECOND BID WAS A JUMP TO 3 NOTRUMP OVER RESPONDER'S FIRST BID OF 2 IN ANY SUIT

If opener has jumped to 3 NT over responder's 2-level suit response, he shows 19-21 high card points with stoppers in all of the unbid suits, regardless of whether responder has shown a new suit (promising at *least* 10 points) or has raised opener's suit (promising at *most* 10 points).

If 3 NT has been bid after responder has raised opener's major suit

Responder should return to four of opener's suit if he has a singleton or void in a side suit, or if he has four or more trumps with two doubletons; otherwise responder should pass 3 NT.

If 3 NT has been bid after responder has raised opener minor suit

Responder should generally pass even if he has a singleton or two doubletons, since the 9-trick game in NT may well make when the 11-trick game in the minor suit cannot.

Examples—After the auction has begun:

Opener	Responder
1♠	2♠
3 NT	

(a)   ♠ A x x x   ♡ x x x   ◊ K x x x x   ♣ x

Responder should return to spades because he has a singleton and four trumps. His ruffing value may well provide two extra tricks.

(b)   ♠ A x x x   ♡ x x   ◊ K x x x   ♣ x x x

Responder should pass 3 NT.

After the auction has begun:

Opener	Responder
1◊	2◊
3 NT	

(c)   ♠ A x x   ♡ x   ◇ K x x x   ♣ x x x x x

Responder should pass.

If opener's 3 NT rebid has followed a two-level new-suit response by responder	Responder should settle for game with 10-11 points, try for slam with 12-13 points, force to a small slam with 14-15 points, try for a grand slam with 16-17 points, and force to a grand slam with 18 points.
With 10-11 points	Responder should bid four of his suit if it is a major and is six or more cards long; or he should bid four of opener's suit if it is a major if he has four-card support or three-card support headed by an honor, and a short suit. Otherwise, he should pass.
With 12-13 points	Responder should try for slam by bidding 4 NT if his hand is balanced; bidding five of opener's suit with an unbalanced hand and four-card support, bidding four of his own suit if it is a minor suit and contains six or more cards and if he has a singleton, or bidding a new suit at the four level. Note that if responder has a 12-13 point hand with a six-card heart suit, his slam try must take the form of a bid in a new suit, since a rebid of four hearts would not promise more than 10 points.

With 14-15 high card points

Responder should jump to 6 NT with a balanced hand. If responder's desire to bid slam is based on distributional values, care should be taken that the partnership is not missing two Aces. Responder should seek to play in six of opener's suit with four-card or longer support and an unbalanced hand, or in six of his own suit with a good six-card suit and an unbalanced hand.

If responder has 14 or more points and/or is uncertain as to which denomination the slam should be played in, he should bid a new suit hoping to gain more information from opener.

Examples—If the auction has commenced:

Opener	Responder
1♠	2◇
3 NT	

(d) ♠ x x   ♡ x x x   ◇ A K Q J x   ♣ x x x

Responder should pass.

(e) ♠ K x x   ♡ x x x   ◇ A x x x   ♣ A x x

Responder should pass.

(f) ♠ x x   ♡ x x   ◇ K Q J x x x   ♣ A x x

Responder should raise to 4 NT.

(g) ♠ Q x x x   ♡ x x   ◇ A K x x x   ♣ J x

Responder should bid 4♠.

(h)   ♠ K x x x   ♡ x   ◇ A x x x x   ♣ K x x

Responder should bid 5 ♠.

(i)   ♠ x x   ♡ A x x   ◇ K Q 10 x x x   ♣ K x

Responder should bid 6 ◇.

(j)   ♠ A x x   ♡ K x x   ◇ A Q x x x   ♣ x x

Responder wants to play in slam but does not know whether the hand will play better in spades, in diamonds, or in NT. He therefore temporizes with a bid of 4♡. If opener bids 4♠ (likely), showing a five-card spade suit, responder can go to 6♠. If opener supports diamonds, responder can go to 6◇. If opener rebids 4 NT, responder can go to 6 NT. If opener raises hearts, responder will go to 6 NT.

REPLIES BY RESPONDER
IF HIS FIRST BID WAS A NEW SUIT AND
OPENER HAS MADE A NON-JUMP RAISE OF THAT SUIT

If responder's initial response was a minor suit at the 2-level, opener's raise shows 16-19 points and the partnership is committed to game. Responder should return to opener's suit if he has three or more cards in that suit, or should bid a new suit if he has another suit, or should bid 3 NT with 10-14 points in a one-suited balanced hand with a doubleton in opener's suit. With 15 or more points, responder should commence to cue-bid in an effort to reach a slam.

If the initial response was a 2♡ over a 1♠ opening, the raise has not shown extra strength and the partnership is not forced to game unless responder rebids.

If responder's initial response was at the one level, opener's raise to two shows 13-16 points. Responder should act as follows:

With 6-10 points   Responder should pass.

With 11-12 points   Responder should make a game try by either rebidding three of his suit with a five-card or longer suit, or bidding 2 NT with the unbid suits stopped, or bidding three of opener's suit with three- or four-card support, or bidding a new suit.

With 13-16 points   Responder should bid game in his suit if it contains five or more cards, or if he has a singleton. Otherwise, he should bid 3 NT.

With 17-19 points   Responder should make a slam try; a cue-bid at this juncture would be temporarily ambiguous, since opener would assume that any new suit bid was an effort to reach game, not slam. Later bidding by responder would clarify his intentions and aspirations.

Examples—If opener has opened with 1♣ and raised a 1♡ response to 2♡ :

(a)   ♠ x x   ♡ A Q x x   ◊ K x x x   ♣ x x x

Responder should pass.

(b)   ♠ K x   ♡ A K x x x   ◇ x x   ♣ x x x x

Responder should bid 3 ♡.

(c)   ♠ K Q x x   ♡ Q J x x   ◇ K x x   ♣ x x

Responder should bid 2 NT.

(d)   ♠ A Q x x   ♡ Q J x x   ◇ A x x   ♣ J x

Responder should bid 3 NT.

(e)   ♠ x   ♡ K Q x x x   ◇ Q x x   ♣ A x x x

Responder should bid 4 ♡.

REPLIES BY RESPONDER
IF HIS FIRST BID WAS ONE IN A SUIT AND
OPENER HAS JUMP-RAISED RESPONDER'S SUIT

If opener has made a jump raise to 3 of responder's suit (showing 17-19 points)

Responder should pass with a bare minimum (6-7 points), but should bid game in his suit with 8-13 points. Any bid in a new suit by responder after opener's jump raise is a cue-bid in search of slam, and shows 14 or more points.

If opener has made a jump raise to 4 of responder's suit (showing 20-21 points)

Responder should pass unless he has 12 or more points. With 12 or more points, responder may cue-bid or use the Blackwood convention.

If opener has made a jump raise to 5 of responder's suit

Opener's rebid asks responder to bid a small slam if he has two of the top three honors in his suit. With the Ace and King, or Ace and Queen, or King and Queen, responder should bid six of his suit.

REPLIES BY RESPONDER
IF OPENER HAS MADE A NON-JUMP REBID
OF HIS OWN SUIT AFTER A NEW SUIT RESPONSE

If opener has made a non-jump rebid in his own suit, he shows a minimum hand worth 13-16 points.

With 6-10 points

Responder should pass.

With 11-12 points and three-card or longer support for opener's suit and a side suit doubleton or singleton

Responder should raise opener's suit to three.

With 11-12 points and a six-card suit, and fewer than three cards in opener's suit

Responder should rebid his suit.

With 11-12 points and with no singleton, and no six-card suit, and fewer than three cards in opener's suit

Responder should bid 2 NT.

With 11-12 points and two five-card suits	Responder should bid his second suit.
With 11-12 points and five spades and four hearts opposite opener's minor suit	Responder should bid 2♡.
With 11-12 points and any other 5-4-3-1, or with 4-4-4-1 distribution with the singleton in opener's suit	Responder should pass.
With 13 or more points	Responder should force to game either by bidding a new suit that ranks higher than his first suit (a reverse), by jumping in his suit, or by bidding a new suit at the three level. Or he can simply jump to game in opener's suit (with three-card or longer support), or jump in his own suit (with a good six-card suit), or in NT.

Examples—After the auction has started:

Opener   Responder
1♡   1♠
2♡

(a)   ♠ A x x x x   ♡ x x x   ◇ K J x   ♣ x x

Responder should pass.

(b)   ♠ K x x x   ♡ K Q x   ◊ A x x   ♣ x x x

Responder should raise to 3 ♡ .

(c)   ♠ K Q x x x   ♡ x   ◊ K x x   ♣ A x x x

Responder should bid 3 ♣ .

(d)   ♠ K Q x x x x   ♡ x   ◊ A x x   ♣ K x x

Responder should bid 3 ♠ .

(e)   ♠ Q x x x x   ♡ x x   ◊ K J x   ♣ A J x

Responder should bid 2 NT.

REPLIES BY RESPONDER IF OPENER HAS JUMPED IN HIS OWN SUIT AFTER A NEW SUIT RESPONSE

If opener has made a jump rebid of 3 of his own suit, he has 17-19 points.

With 6-7 points	Responder should pass. Any rebid by responder is forcing to game.
With 8-13 points, if the opening bid was in a major suit and responder has two or more cards in the suit	Responder should raise to game in opener's suit unless his points consist principally of Queens and Jacks; with Queens and Jacks and a stopper in the unbid major suit, responder should rebid 3 NT.

With 8-13 points, if the opening bid was in a minor suit Responder should make a reasonable effort to see that 3 NT is reached. If he lacks the requisite major suit stoppers for 3 NT, he can either rebid his suit if it is at least five cards long, bid a new suit, or raise opener.

Examples—If the auction has begun:

Opener	Responder
1♡	1♠
3♡	

(a)   ♠ Q x x x   ♡ x x   ◊ K x x   ♣ Q x x x

Responder should pass.

(b)   ♠ Q x x x x x   ♡ x   ◊ x x   ♣ K x x

Responder should pass.

(c)   ♠ K Q x x   ♡ x x   ◊ x x x   ♣ A x x x

Responder should raise to 4♡.

(d)   ♠ K Q x x x   ♡ x   ◊ Q x x x   ♣ x x x

Responder should bid 3♠.

If instead the auction had started:

Opener	Responder
1◊	1♠
3◊	

Responder should raise to 4◇ with hand (c), for lack of a better bid, and should rebid 3♠ with hand (d), hoping opener can either raise spades or rebid 3 NT.

If opener has jumped to game in his own suit, that bid shows 20-21 points.

If responder has 6-11 points, he should pass. Any bid by responder over opener's jump to game is a slam try and promises 12 or more points.

REPLIES BY RESPONDER
IF OPENER HAS BID A NEW SUIT OVER
RESPONDER'S INITIAL RESPONSE IN A NEW SUIT

After a non-reverse rebid of a new suit by opener at the one level, or at the two level in a suit that ranks lower than opener's first suit, showing 13-18 points, as in the following auctions:

(a)	Opener	Responder	(b)	Opener	Responder
	1♣	1♡		1♡	1♠
	1♠			2◇	

(c)	Opener	Responder
	1♠	2♣
	2♡	

responder should not count on opener to have more than 13-15 points. On that assumption, responder should sign off with 6-10 points, invite game with 11-12 points, and force to game with 13-15 points.

Any non-jump rebid by responder in a new suit forces opener to bid once more. Such a bid by responder has no upper point count limit.

Any jump rebid by responder, or any reverse (i.e., a non-jump bid in a new suit that prevents opener from returning to responder's first bid suit at the two level), forces opener to continue bidding until game is reached.

After a new suit bid by opener as in the auctions above, responder should take the following actions. Note that a hand worth 11-12 points is sometimes awkward to bid after a response at the one level, often requiring an underbid, an overbid, or a bid in a suit of fewer than four cards.

If responder has four or more cards in opener's first suit and does not have greater length in opener's second suit	He should return to opener's first suit: at the two level with 6-10 points, or by jumping with 13 or more points. With 11-12 points, responder should bid 2 NT if he has a stopper in the unbid suit and if opener's second bid was at the *two level;* otherwise, responder should bid the unbid suit if he can do so without reversing, or raise opener's suit.
If responder has four or more cards in opener's second suit, and fewer cards in opener's first suit	If opener has rebid at the one level as in auction (a) above, responder should pass with 6 points, or raise opener's second suit to the two level with 7-10 points, or jump in the suit with 13 or more points. With 11-12 points, responder should bid 2 NT if he has a stopper in the unbid suit and if opener's second bid was at the *two level;* otherwise, responder

should bid the unbid suit if he can do so without reversing, or raise opener's second suit.

If opener has bid at the two level, responder should pass if he has less than 10 points, or raise to the three level with 10-12 points; or force to game with 13 or more points (if opener's second suit is a minor, responder should usually force by bidding a new suit rather than by jumping, to avoid bypassing 3 NT).

If responder does not have four-card support for either or opener's suits, but has a six-card or longer suit of his own

He should rebid his suit without jumping if he has 8-12 points, or by jumping if he has 13 or more points. With 6-7 points, responder should usually take a preference for one of opener's suits.

If responder has five or more cards in the unbid suit

If he has 13 or more points, he should bid the suit. If he has 10-12 points, he should bid the suit only if he can do so without reversing; if he cannot, he should either rebid his first suit if it is six cards long, or bid whichever of opener's suits he prefers. If he has 6-9 points, he should take a preference for one of opener's suits by bidding the first, or by passing, or rebid 1 NT.

If responder has 5-4-3-1 distribution with the tripleton and the singleton in opener's suits

If responder has 6-9 points, he should express his preference for the suit in which he has three cards in the same manner as he would show four-card support. If responder has 10-12 points, he should either bid the unbid suit if he can do so without reversing, or bid 2 NT if opener's rebid was at the two level; otherwise, he should raise whichever of opener's suits he prefers. If responder has 13 or more points, he should bid the unbid suit.

If responder has a balanced hand with length or a stopper in the unbid suit, and without four-card support for either of opener's suits

If opener has rebid at the one level (e.g., as in auction (a) above), responder should, with one exception, bid 1 NT with 7-10 points, or jump to 2 NT with 13-15 points. The one exception is that if the auction has started 1♣-1◇-1♡, and responder has four spades, he should bid 1♠. If responder has 11-12 points, he should bid the unbid suit if he can do so without reversing; otherwise he should raise whichever of opener's suits he prefers. With 6 points, responder should take a preference for one of opener's suits by returning to the first suit or by passing.

If opener has rebid at the two level (e.g., as in auctions (b) or (c) above),

responder should rebid 2 NT with
10-12 points, or 3 NT with 13-15
points. If responder has 6-9 points
(having responded initially at the
one level as in auction (b), he should
simply take a preference for one of
opener's suits.

If opener has shown 17 or more points by bidding his new suit at
the three level after a two-level response, the partnership is commit-
ed to game. Responder should bid naturally, bidding opener's suit if
he has four-card or longer support, rebidding his own suit if it
contains six or more cards, bidding NT with a stopper in the unbid
suit, or bidding a new suit. Responder should try for slam with 14-15
points.

If opener has shown 19 or more points by reversing (i.e., bidding
a suit at the two level that is higher ranking than his first suit),
responder should make every effort to bid again, despite the fact
that, if responder's initial response was at the one level, the reverse is
not forcing. Unless responder has a strong preference for opener's
second suit and has even less than the 6 points promised by his first
response, he should bid again. *If responder bids, opener is forced to
bid again.*

Examples:

(d)   ♠ K x x x   ♡ A K x x x x   ◇ x   ♣ x x

*If opener has opened 1♣ and has bid 1♠ over responder's
1♡, responder should jump to 3♠, showing four spades in a
game-forcing hand.*

(e) ♠ K Q x x x x   ♥ x   ♦ x x x   ♣ A x x

If opener has opened 1♥ and has bid 2♦ over responder's 1♠, responder should rebid 2♠. He does not have enough strength to jump in his suit or to go to the three level by bidding 3♣.

(f) ♠ Q x   ♥ K Q x x   ♦ x x x   ♣ A J x x

If opener has opened 1♦ and has bid 1♠ over responder's 1♥, responder has just the wrong strength to bid NT, since 1 NT would show a maximum of 10 and 2 NT would show a minimum of 13. Responder should bid 2♣. Had opener opened with 1♠ and bid 2♦ over a 2♣ response, responder would have had an automatic bid of 2 NT.

(g) ♠ Q x x x   ♥ A x x x x   ♦ J x   ♣ Q x

(h) ♠ J x   ♥ A x x x x   ♦ Q x x x   ♣ Q x

If opener has opened 1♦ and has bid 2♣ over a 1♥ response, responder should bid 2♦ with both hands (g) and (h). If opener has opened with 1♣, however, and rebid 1♠ over the 1♥ response, responder should rebid 2♠ with hand (g) and 1 NT with hand (h).

(i) ♠ x   ♥ K x x x x   ♦ x x   ♣ Q J x x x

If opener has opened 1♦ and has bid 1♠ over responder's 1♥, responder should bid 1 NT. He lacks the requisite strength to introduce another new suit, which would force opener to bid again.

(j) ♠ x x   ♥ K Q x x   ♦ A Q x x x   ♣ x x

If opener has opened 1♠ and has bid 3♣ over responder's

2◊ , responder should bid 3NT. He should not bid hearts, since he does not have more strength than he has already shown. And opener is not likely to have four hearts, since he did not bid them.

(k)   ♠ K x x x   ♡ x x   ◊ K x x   ♣ x x x x

If opener has opened 1◊ and has bid 2♡ over responder's 1♠, responder should bid 3◊ .

REPLIES BY RESPONDER
IF OPENER'S SECOND BID WAS A JUMP IN A NEW SUIT

After opener has jumped in a new suit, responder is forced to continue bidding until game has been reached. He should rebid according to the priorities set forth below. In making any of the suit bids described below, it is unnecessary for responder to jump, even with a very strong hand, since the partnership is already forced to game.

If responder has four-card or longer support for opener's first suit, or if he has a weak hand with Q x or better in opener's first suit, he should bid that suit.

If responder has no more than three cards in opener's first suit and has a good six-card or longer suit of his own (K Q x x x x or better), he should rebid his suit.

If responder has four-card support for opener's second suit and worse than four cards or Q x in opener's first suit, and has no good six-card suit, he should raise opener's second suit.

If responder has no good six-card suit of his own and has fewer than four cards in opener's second suit, but has three card support for opener's first suit, he should bid opener's first suit.

If responder has no good six-card or longer suit of his own and has fewer than three cards in opener's first suit and fewer than four cards in opener's second suit, he should bid NT unless he has a worthless doubleton in the unbid suit; with such a worthless doubleton, responder should show a "false" preference for opener's first suit.

OPENER'S THIRD BID

If the bidding has progressed through a second bid by responder, opener can re-evaluate his hand to discount his shortness in suits bid by responder and be encouraged by length and honors in such suits. Opener then generally knows whether the partnership should stop in a part-score or reach game or try for slam.

OPENER'S THIRD BID IF RESPONDER
HAS NOT PROMISED MORE THAN 10 POINTS

If responder has not promised more than 10 points, and has not made a forcing bid in a new suit at his second turn, opener should sign off if he has 13-16 points. His goal is to have the partnership rest in a suit in which it has a total of 8 or more cards, or in NT. He signs off as follows:

If Opener has 13-16 points:

And has a balanced hand (4-3-3-3, 4-4-3-2, 5-3-3-2, or 5-4-2-2)	Opener should pass if responder's second bid was 1 NT, or a rebid of responder's suit, or a bid in one of opener's suits.

If responder's second bid was in a new suit at the one level, i.e., the auction has started:

Opener	Responder
1♣	1♢
1♡	1♠

opener should bid 1 NT.

If responder's second bid was in a new suit at the two level (in a suit ranking lower than the suit of his first response) over opener's second bid of 1 NT, opener should take a preference for one of responder's suits, either by passing with greater length in responder's second suit, or by returning to responder's first suit.

And he has a seven-card suit	If responder has rebid his suit and opener has two-card or longer support, and opener's own suit is weak, opener should pass. Otherwise, opener should rebid his suit.
And he has a six-card suit and no second suit with more than four cards	Opener should pass if responder has rebid his own suit or has taken a preference for one of opener's suits. Otherwise, opener should rebid his six-card suit.
And he has a hand with two suits, each containing five or more cards	Opener should pass if responder has rebid his own suit or has taken a preference for one of opener's suits. Otherwise, opener should rebid his second suit.

And he has 5-4-3-1 or 4-4-4-1 distribution

Opener should pass if responder has rebid his own suit or has taken a preference for one of opener's suits.

If responder has rebid 1 NT, opener should return to responder's suit if his singleton is in the unbid suit; opener should pass 1 NT if his singleton is in responder's suit.

If responder has bid a new suit at the one level, i.e., the auction has started:

Opener	Responder
1♣	1♦
1♡	1♠

opener should raise the suit bid by responder in which he has the greater length.

Examples:

(a)

Opener	Responder
1♣	1♡
1♠	2♣, 2♡, or 2♠

If opener has 13-15 points, he should pass any of responder's second bids. If responder instead had bid 2♦, opener would be forced to bid again.

(b)

Opener	Responder
1♦	1♠
1 NT	

Opener should pass if responder's second bid is 2♦ or 2♠. If responder bids 2♣ or 2♡ on his second bid, opener should express a preference for one of responder's suits, either by passing or returning to responder's first suit.

(c)   Opener   Responder
        1◊   1♡
        1♠   1 NT

If opener has a hand such as:

♠ K x x x   ♡ x   ◊ K Q x x   ♣ A x x x

he should pass.

If responder has promised 6-10 points and opener has 17-18 points, opener should bid a third time to invite responder to bid game if he holds 9-10 points, unless he has *already* made an invitation that has been rejected.

Examples:

(d)   Opener   Responder
        1♣   1♡
        1♠   1 NT
        2 NT

Opener has not shown extra strength with his first or second bid. Thus when responder bids 1 NT, opener may invite game if he has 17-18 points.

(e)   Opener   Responder
        1♠   2♣
        3◊   3♠
        Pass

Opener has made a game try with his second bid; if he has no more than 18 points, he has nothing more to say when responder signs off at 3♠.

In making his game try with 17-18 points, opener should bear in mind that game in a minor suit (needing 29 points) is a remote chance, and should select the type of game invitation that is most likely to land the partnership in a major suit contract if there are a total of at least 8 hearts or spades between the two hands, or in NT if there are adequate stoppers in the unbid suits. The guidelines are as follows:

If Opener has 17-18 points:

And he has a balanced hand (4-3-3-3, or 4-4-3-2, or 5-3-3-2, or 5-4-2-2)	Opener should bid 2 NT if responder's second bid was 1 NT or a new suit, or if responder's second bid was in one of opener's suits and opener has the unbid suit stopped.
	If responder has rebid his own suit, opener should raise responder's suit.
And he has a six-card suit and no second suit of more than four cards	If responder has rebid his own suit, opener should raise responder's suit if he has two-card or longer support; otherwise, he should bid 2 NT with the unbid suits stopped, or bid three of his long suit.
And he has a hand with two suits, each containing five or more cards	Opener should rebid his second suit, unless he has a doubleton or tripleton in responder's suit and responder has rebid the suit, in which case opener should raise responder's suit.

And he has 5-4-3-1 or 4-4-4-1 distribution

If responder has rebid 1 NT, opener should raise to 2 NT if his singleton is in responder's suit, or should *jump raise* responder's suit if his singleton is in the unbid suit.

If responder has rebid his suit, opener should raise if he has a singleton in the unbid suit, or should bid NT if his singleton is in responder's suit.

If responder has taken a preference for one of opener's suits, opener should raise the suit preferred by responder if it is a major suit; if it is a minor, opener should rebid in NT if his singleton is in responder's suit, or should raise responder's suit if his singleton is in the unbid suit.

If responder has bid a new suit at the one level, i.e., the bidding has started:

Opener	Responder
1♣	1◇
1♡	1♠

opener should jump to 2 NT unless he has four spades, in which case, he should jump to 3♠.

If opener has 19-20 points and has not jump-shifted or reversed at his second turn, he should jump to game at his third term.

Example:

(f)   ♠ A J x x   ♡ A K x x   ◇ x   ♣ K Q x x

If the auction has started:

Opener	Responder
1♣	1◇
1♡	1♠

opener should jump to 4♠.

If opener has reversed and responder has rebid, opener is forced to bid again. His options are to support responder's suit with three or more cards, to bid NT with the unbid suits stopped (or to raise in NT with a balanced hand if responder has bid NT), or to rebid one of his own suits.

OPENER'S THIRD BID
IF RESPONDER HAS SHOWN 11-12 POINTS

If responder has shown 11-12 points without making a forcing rebid, opener should sign off is he has 13 points or a bad 14 points. He signs off by rebidding one of his suits, if neither has been supported, or by passing.

Examples:

(a) | Opener | Responder |
|--------|-----------|
| 1♡ | 2♣ |
| 2◇ | 2 NT |

Opener's rebid of 3◇ or 3♡ over 2 NT would be a sign off.

(b)   *Opener*   *Responder*
          1♡   1♠
          2♣   3♣

To sign off, opener would pass. A 3♡ bid by him at his third turn would be forcing since responder has supported opener's other suit.

If opener has a good 14-20 points, he should bid game or force to game. He should take care not to rebid his suit in an auction such as (a) above, since this amounts to a sign off.

If opener knows that the partnership has no more than 27 points, he should aim toward game in a major suit or in NT, rather than in a minor.

Opener's options are to bid game in one of his suits or in responder's suit if an eight-card fit has been located, or in NT if opener has stoppers in the unbid suits (or if he has a balanced hand and responder has bid NT).

If responder has made a forcing bid in a new suit at each turn, e.g.,

(c)   *Opener*   *Responder*
          1♣   1♡
          1♠   2♢

opener should show a preference if he has three-card or longer support for responder's suits. Without such support for one of responder's suits, opener may bid NT with balanced distribution or rebid one of his own suits with five or more cards and unbalanced distribution.

If opener has 21 or more points, he should invite slam.

OPENER'S THIRD BID
IF RESPONDER HAS BID GAME OR FORCED TO GAME

If responder has bid game or forced to game at his second turn, showing 13-16 points, opener should settle for game without trying for slam if he has 13-16 points. Opener's method of settling for game depends on what type of game force responder has used.

If responder has jumped in opener's major suit	Opener should bid four of his suit.
If responder has jumped in opener's minor suit	Opener should bid 3 NT with the unbid suits stopped.
If responder has made a jump rebid in his own major suit	Opener should raise to game in that suit if he has two-card or longer support. Otherwise, opener should rebid one of his own suits, or bid NT with the unbid suits stopped.
If responder has made a jump rebid in his own minor suit	Opener should bid 3 NT with the unbid suits stopped.
If responder has jumped in NT	Opener should settle for 3 NT if he has a relatively balanced hand or if his only short suit is one bid by responder. If opener has an unbalanced hand with three-card support for responder's major suit, he should return to responder's suit. If opener has ten or more cards in his own two suits, he

should rebid one of his suits (the longer if he is 6-4, or the second if he is 5-5 or longer).

If responder has bid two suits, and has jumped or reversed on his second bid

Opener should either support responder's first suit if he has three or more cards in that suit, or support responder's second suit if he has four cards in that suit. Lacking such support, opener should bid NT unless he has 10 or more cards in two suits. If opener has ten or more cards in his own two suits, he should rebid one of his suits.

If opener holds 17 or more points opposite responder's game force, he should try for slam.

RESPONDER'S THIRD BID

By the time responder must make his third bid of the auction, he generally knows opener's strength within 2-3 points. He also usually knows opener's distribution within 1-2 cards. For example, if opener has bid three suits, he usually has a singleton or a void in the fourth suit.

In determining what action to take at his third turn, responder should re-evaluate his hand to discount shortness in the suits bid by opener and to promote the honors he holds in opener's suits. He should also tend to discount any Queens and Jacks he hold in suits in which opener is known to hold few cards, unless he plans to steer the hand into NT.

RESPONDER'S THIRD BID
OVER A SIGN-OFF BY OPENER

Over a sign-off bid by opener on the third round, responder should generally pass unless he has at least 11-12 points, i.e., enough for game if opener has 15 points.

If responder's third bid is in hearts or spades, it invites opener to bid game in that suit with 15-16 points. If responder's third bid is in clubs or diamonds, it also invites opener to bid game with 15-16 points, but NT should be given primary consideration since game in a minor suit normally requires 29 points.

RESPONDER'S THIRD BID
AFTER OPENER HAS INVITED GAME

If responder, by his first two bids, has not promised more than 10 points, a game invitation by opener asks him to bid game if he has 9-10 points. If he has 6-8 points, he should sign off, normally by passing.

If responder has promised 11-12 points, a game invitation by opener asks responder to bid game with 12 points, or to sign off with 11.

In accepting a game invitation by opener, responder should tend to bid 3 NT or four of a major suit rather than 5♣ or 5◇, since generally more points are needed for the minor suit game.

RESPONDER'S THIRD BID
AFTER OPENER HAS BID A GAME

After opener has bid a game at his third turn, responder should pass unless he has enought points to invite a slam.

Responder should calculate how many points opener has promised by his first three bids. He should re-evaluate his own hand to promote honors in opener's suits and to devalue shortness in those suits. When responder adds his own points to those shown by opener, if the total could reach 33 points if opener has a maximum, responder should bid toward slam.

Examples—If the auction has started:

Opener	Responder
1♢	1♡
1 NT	3♣
3 NT	

responder knows that opener has a balanced hand with 13-15 points. Opener probably has no more than three spades, and no more than two hearts. His most likely distribution is three spades, two hearts, five diamonds, and three clubs. If responder holds:

(a)   ♠ Ax   ♡ KQxxx   ♢ x   ♣ Axxxx

Responder should pass 3 NT.

(b)   ♠ —   ♡ AKxxx   ♢ Qxx   ♣ AKxxx

Responder has enough strength and enough diamonds to insist on a diamond slam.

(c)   ♠ x   ♡ AKxx   ♢ Qxxx   ♣ AQxx

Responder should bid 4♢, inviting a diamond slam. The 4♢ bid cannot be passed, and it suggests that responder has a singleton or void in spades, allowing opener to evaluate his hand further.

(d)   ♠ K Q J   ♡ Q x   ◇ A J x x x   ♣ x x x

If opener held this hand after a 4 ◇ third bid by responder in the above auction, opener would sign off in 4 NT, since so many of his values are wasted in spades.

(e)   ♠ A x x   ♡ x x   ◇ A K x x x   ♣ K x x

If opener held this hand after a 4 ◇ third bid by responder in the above auction, opener should see to it that slam is reached. He should start by cue-bidding 4 ♠ .

EFFECTS OF OPPONENT'S INTERVENTION ON RESPONSES AND REBIDS AFTER AN OPENING IN A SUIT

After an opponent has entered the auction, certain of the responses and rebids of the side that opened the bidding take on different meanings. In addition, new types of bids become available.

MEANINGS OF RESPONSES AND REBIDS AFTER AN OPPONENT'S OVERCALL IN A SUIT

In general, responder's raise of opener's suit and opener's raise of responder's suit retain their original meanings after an overcall. These raises do not promise any extra strength. In addition, they may be made more frequently with three-card support rather than four-card support.

Examples:

	North	East	South	West
(a)	1♠	2♣	2♠	
(b)	1◇	Pass	1♠	2♡
	2♠			
(c)	1♣	1◇	1♡	2◇
	2♡			

The raise by South in auction (a) and those by North in auctions (b) and (c) do not show extra values.

Responses and bids in new suits or in NT made directly over an overcall generally show somewhat greater strength than they would without intervention.

A NT response over an overcall promises 9-12 points with a stopper in the suit overcalled.

A NT rebid by opener directly over an overcall shows better than a minimum opening. If the overcall was on opener's left, he may have only 14 or 15 points.

Examples:

	North	East	South	West
(d)	1♣	1♡	1 NT	
(e)	1◇	Pass	1♡	1♠
	1 NT			

South's 1 NT response promises 9-12 points.

Opener's NT bid promises at least 15 points.

(f)   1♡   Pass   1♠   2♣
        2 NT

Opener's NT bid promises better than a minimum opening bid. Since he has bid at the two level, he should have at least 16 points.

(g)   1◇   1♡   1♠   Pass
        1 NT

Opener may have as little as 14 points for his 1 NT bid.

Responses in new suits directly over suit overcalls also promise extra strength.

If responder freely bids a new suit at the one level over the overcall, he promises at least 9 points.

If he bids a new suit at the two level over the overcall, he promises at least 11 points, or even more if his suit ranks higher than opener's suit, making it impossible for opener to return to his suit at the two level.

All responses that would be forcing without intervention retain their forcing character afte an overcall in a suit.

If opener rebids at the one level after an overcall by his right-hand opponent, he does not promise more than 14 points.

If opener rebids at the two level after an overcall he shows extra values, although not necessarily more than 16 points.

Example:

(a)   *North*   *East*   *South*   *West*
       1◇   Pass   1♡   2♣
       2♠

Opener's 2♠ bid shows extra values, but is not a true reverse, since if West had not intervened, opener would have been able to rebid 1♠, allowing responder to return to diamonds at the two level.

MEANINGS OF RESPONSES
AFTER AN OPPONENT'S NOTRUMP OVERCALL

If the overcall has been 1 NT, a response in a new suit does not promise, and in fact denies, extra strength. **Such a response is not forcing.**

The only strong actions after a 1 NT opercall are a double promising 9 points, and seeking to penalize the overcaller, and a cue-bid of 2 NT showing a strong two-suited hand.

Examples—After the auction has started:

North	East	South	West
1◊	1 NT		

(a)   ♠ xx   ♡ A J x x x   ◊ x x x   ♣ x x x

South should bid 2♡.

(b)   ♠ K x x   ♡ A x x x   ◊ x x   ♣ J x x x

South should pass.

(c)   ♠ x x x x   ♡ K J x   ◊ Q x x   ♣ A x x

South should double.

(d)   ♠ K Q x x x x   ♡ x   ◊ —   ♣ A x x x x x

South should bid 2 NT.

DOUBLE OF OPPONENT'S OVERCALL

A double by responder of an opponent's overcall is a penalty double. It promises good trumps and a hand worth at least a game invitation.

A double by opener of an opponent's overcall is a takeout double if responder has *not* yet bid. If responder *has* bid, opener's double is for penalties. The penalty double promises a hand worth at least a game invitation opposite the range of strength shown by responder's response.

CUE-BID OF OPPONENT'S OVERCALL

The cue-bid of a suit in which an opponent has overcalled generally shows a very strong hand.

Although the cue-bid may mean any of a number of things, it is usually forcing to game. The circumstances in which the cue-bid is not necessarily forcing to game are those in which one member of the partnership has already passed and thereby limited his hand.

Examples:

(a) | *North* | *East* | *South* | *West* |
|---|---|---|---|
| 1♡ | Pass | Pass | 1♠ |
| 2♠ | | | |

North's 2♠ cue-bid is not game forcing because North has not opened with a forcing two-bid and South has passed the opening bid, showing 0-6 points.

(b)

North	East	South	West
1 ◇	Pass	1 ♠	2 ♣
Pass	Pass	3 ♣	

South's 3♣ cue-bid is not game forcing because North has probably shown a minimum by failing to make a free bid over West's 2♣ overcall.

The meaning of a cue-bid in a suit overcalled by an opponent depends in part on the level at which the cue-bid is made. If made at the four level or higher, the cue-bid promises control of the opponent's suit and shows slam interest.

If the cue-bid is made at a lower level before a trump suit has been agreed upon, it can mean either that the cue-bidder is not sure in which denomination to play, or that the hand is too strong for a simple rebid of his own suit or a raise of opener's suit.

In the latter event, the cue-bidder will follow up with a rebid or raise on the next round, and his cue-bid will have shown at least second-round control of the opponent's suit. If the cue-bid is made because the cue-bidder does not know in which denomination to play, his cue-bid does not promise control of the opponent's suit.

Examples:

North	East	South	West
1 ◇	Pass	1 ♠	2 ♡
3 ♡	Pass	3 NT	Pass

North's cue-bid of 3♡ is ambiguous. If he has a hand such as:

(c)   ♠ x x   ♡ x x   ◇ A K Q J x x   ♣ A x x

he will pass 3 NT.

If he has such a hand as:

(d)   ♠ A K x x   ♡ x   ◇ A K Q x x x   ♣ K x

*he will bid 4♠ over 3 NT, revealing a hand that was too
strong for a simple jump to 4♠ over 2♡.*

In response to the low level cue-bid, cue-bidder's partner should
make whatever bid he considers will be most useful. If he has a
stopper in the opponent's suit, he should bid NT. Lacking a stopper,
he should bid his own suit if it is at least five cards long and headed
by a high honor, or support his partner's suit if he has three or more
cards, or bid a new suit.

The opportunity to cue-bid an opponent's suit has an effect on
the meaning of a jump to five of a major suit that has been agreed as
trumps. If the opportunity to cue-bid has been bypassed, the jump
to five of the suit agreed as trumps asks partner to bid six with
second-round control of the opponent's suit. If the cue-bid was
made, the jump retains its ordinary meaning.

MEANINGS OF RESPONSES AND REBIDS
AFTER AN OPPONENT'S TAKEOUT DOUBLE

After an opponent's takeout double, the meanings of many of responder's bids are sharply altered. Responses in a new suit *are no
longer forcing.*

The only strong response is a redouble, promising at least 10
points.

Raises, the 1 NT response, and bids in a new suit show less than
10 points.

A 1 NT response over an opponent's takeout double promises 7-9
points.

A raise of opener's suit to the two level shows 5-9 points, and may be made purely for the purpose of pre-empting with a weak hand.

A raise to the three level promises the same high card strength, but it is solely pre-emptive; it is generally based on uneven distribution, with a side suit singleton or void. A raise to the four level is similarly distributional and pre-emptive—only more so.

A response in a new suit at the one level promises at least a five-card suit and less than 10 points.

A response in a new suit at the two level normally shows a six-card suit and less than 10 points.

A bid by opener in a new suit after a takeout double does not show extra strength if responder has bid, but does show extra strength if responder has not bid.

RESPONDER'S REDOUBLE OF OPPONENT'S TAKEOUT DOUBLE

After the takeout double, a redouble by responder promises at least 10 points and asks opener to pass unless he has a very distributional hand. The redouble is responder's only way to show a strong hand after an opponent's takeout double.

Responder intends to clarify his hand at his next turn. He may make a penalty double of the suit bid by the opponents after his redouble; or with four-card support for opener's suit, he may make a simple raise of opener's suit with 10-11 points or a jump raise (forcing to game) with 12-13 points.

With a balanced hand and a stopper in any suit bid by an opponent, but without support for opener's suit, responder may bid NT—the minimum number with 10-11 points, or a jump with 12-13 (forcing to game); or responder may bid a new suit. The new suit bid forces opener to bid once more.

Examples—If the auction has begun:

North	East	South	West
1♡	Double	Redouble	Pass
Pass	2♣		

(a)   ♠ K x x x   ♡ x   ◇ A x x x   ♣ A Q x x

South should make a penalty double of 2♣.

(b)   ♠ Q x x   ♡ x x   ◇ A 10 x x x   ♣ A Q x

South should jump to 3 NT.

(c)   ♠ A x x   ♡ x   ◇ A Q x x x x   ♣ A x x

South should bid 2◇.

(d)   ♠ x x x x   ♡ A x x x   ◇ A Q x   ♣ x x

South should raise opener's hearts to 2♡.

(e)   ♠ Q x x x   ♡ K x x x   ◇ A Q x   ♣ K x

South should jump raise opener's hearts to 3♡.

OPENER'S REDOUBLE OF OPPONENT'S TAKEOUT DOUBLE

A redouble by opener of a takeout double after a response, as in the auction:

North	East	South	West
1◇	Pass	1♡	Double
Redouble			

promises extra strength. It does not necessarily guarantee length in responder's suit. However, if opener has length, he can raise responder's suit at his next turn.

Examples:

(a) ♠ J x x   ♡ x x   ◇ A K Q x x x   ♣ A K

(b) ♠ A x   ♡ K J x   ◇ A K x x x   ♣ K x x

(c) ♣ x x   ♡ Q x x   ◇ A K x x x   ♣ A x x

For his redouble, opener might have either hand (a) or (b). With hand (c), however, he would simply raise responder's hearts at once over the double.

A redouble by opener when his righthand opponent has made a balancing double also promises extra strength, as in the auction:

North	East	South	West
1♡	Pass	Pass	Double
Redouble			

Here opener shows substantially better than a minimum opening bid, with a long strong heart suit and good defensive strength.

Examples:

(d) ♠ K x   ♡ A K J x x   ◇ A Q x x   ♣ K x

Appropriate for opener's redouble.

(e) ♠ K x   ♡ A K J x x x x   ◇ A x   ♣ x x

Opener should not redouble because he lacks defensive strength. His hand is strong because of his playing values, and he should invite game by jumping to 3♡.

MEANINGS OF RESPONSES
AFTER AN OPPONENT'S CUE-BID

After an opponent has made a cue-bid in opener's or responder's suit, bids by opener and responder are affected in the same way that they are affected by a natural overcall—that is, raises do not show extra values, but bids in NT and new suits do show additional strength.

Examples:

North	East	South	West
1♣(a)	2♣	3♣	

Responder's 3♣ bid is the equivalent of a raise to 2♣ without competition.

1♡(b)	2♡	2NT	
1◇(c)	2◇	2♡	

In the auctions (b) and (c), responder promises at least an 11 point hand.

DOUBLE OF OPPONENT'S CUE-BID

The double of an opponent's cue-bid is for penalties and is similar to the double of an overcall.

Openings of
2 of a Suit

Opening bids of two of a suit are the only forcing openings in the Standard American style of bidding. These bids force responder to respond and to keep the bidding open until game is reached or the opponents have been doubled for penalties.

STRENGTH REQUIRED
TO BID 2 OF A SUIT

The requirements for a forcing two-bid are as follows:

    25 points with a good five-card suit.

    23 points with a good six-card suit.

    21 points with a good seven-card suit.

    With a second good suit of five cards, one point less is needed.

Examples:

    (a)   ♠ A x   ♡ A K J x x x   ◇ K Q J x x   ♣ —
    Should be opened 2♡.

169

(b)   ♠ K J x   ♡ x   ◊ A K Q J x   ♣ A K Q x

Should be opened 2 ◊ .

RESPONSES TO FORCING TWO BIDS

No matter how weak his hand may be, responder must respond to any opening bid of two in a suit.

NEGATIVE RESPONSE OF 2 NOTRUMP

With a weak hand, responder's proper bid is normally 2 NT, regardless of his distribution. The range of the 2 NT response is usually 0-6 points.

No matter how weak his hand, responder must, except in one sequence, respond to any *rebid* by opener until game is reached or until the opponents are doubled for penalties. The only sequence that is not forcing to game after an opening forcing two-bid is that in which responder makes the negative response of 2 NT and opener simply rebids three of his original suit. In this sequence, responder need not bid again unless he has four or more points.

Example:

(a)   *Opener   Responder*
          2♡   2 NT
          3♡

If he has 0-3 points, responder is allowed to pass in this auction. He should bid again, however, if he has 4-6 points.

With 9 or more high card points, or with 7-8 high card points and a good suit, or with Q x x x or better in opener's suit, responder should not make the negative response of 2 NT.

RAISE OF OPENER'S SUIT TO THREE

The raise of opener's suit to three shows at least three-card support for opener's suit and a minimum of 7-8 points with at least ½ quick trick.

If the raise is made with only 7 points, the hand should contain at least one quick trick. This raise agrees on opener's suit as trumps, and suggests that responder has an Ace, a King, a void or a singleton he can cue-bid later.

Examples—After an opening 2♠ bid:

(a)   ♠ Q x x   ♡ x   ◇ A x x x   ♣ x x x x x

Responder should raise to 3♠.

(b)   ♠ J x x   ♡ x   ◇ K x x x   ♣ x x x x x

This hand is too weak for a raise. Responder should first bid 2 NT and then support spades on the next round.

RAISE OF OPENER'S SUIT TO FOUR

A jump raise of opener's suit shows good trumps—Q x x x (or even longer trumps, with or without the Queen)—but denies an Ace or a King or a void or a singleton. The hand may be very weak except for its trump holding.

Example:

(a)   ♠ Q x x x   ♡ x x   ◇ x x x   ♣ x x x x

Responder should raise a 2♠ opening to 4♠.

RESPONSE IN A NEW SUIT

The bid of a new suit by responder promises a suit of at least five cards headed by at least the Queen and Jack, in a hand worth at least 7 high card points with 1 quick trick or at least 8 high card points with ½ quick trick.

Example:

(a)   ♠ x x   ♡ x x   ◇ K x x x x   ♣ K J x x

*Responder should bid 3 ◇ over an opening bid of 2 ♠ or 2 ♡.
He should bid 2 ◇ over a 2 ♣ opening.*

RESPONSE OF 3 NOTRUMP

A jump response of 3 NT promises 8-9 points with fewer than three cards in opener's suit and without a suit as good as five cards headed by the Queen and Jack.

Example:

(a)   ♠ x x   ♡ A J x   ◇ Q x x x   ♣ Q x x x

Facing an opening bid of 2 ♠, this hand is worth a jump to 3 NT. However, if the opening two-bid were in any other suit, responder would raise opener's suit to three.

ACE SHOWING BY AGREEMENT

By special agreement of the partnership, the responses to an opening two-bid may be altered to require responder to show his Aces. A 2 NT response means that responder has no Aces. If responder has one Ace, he bids the suit of his Ace. If responder has two Aces, he jumps in the suit of his lower ranking Ace.

Example:

(a)   ♠ xx   ♡ Axx   ◊ KQJxxxx   ♣ x

In response to a forcing 2♠ opening, responder would bid 3♡.

REBIDS BY OPENER AND RESPONDER AFTER FORCING TWO BID

If opener has a one-suited hand, he should simply rebid his suit.

If the response has been 2 NT and opener has a probable 10 tricks in his own hand, he should take care to jump, for the non-jump rebid in this sequence would not be forcing.

If opener has a 9-trick hand, he should make the non-jump rebid after a 2 NT response. Responder, if he has a maximum for his negative response, that is, 4 or more points, will continue to game—either in opener's suit or in NT.

Examples—After the auction has commenced 2♠-2 NT:

(a)   ♠ AKQxxxxx   ♡ Ax   ◊ A   ♣ xx

Opener should bid 4♠.

(b)   ♠ AKQxxxx   ♡ Ax   ◊ Axx   ♣ x

Opener should bid 3♠.

(c)   ♠ xx   ♡ Kxxx   ◇ xxxx   ♣ Jxx

If opener has opened 2♠ and rebid 3♠, responder should raise to 4♠.

(d)   ♠ x   ♡ Qxxx   ◇ Qxxx   ♣ xxxx

If opener has opened 2♠ and rebid 3♠, responder should rebid 3 NT.

Any rebid by opener of his suit precludes agreement on any other suit as trumps.

Thus, after opener has rebid his suit, any other suit bid by either opener or responder is a cue-bid in search of slam.

Examples:

(e)   Opener   Responder
      2♡   2♠
      3♡   3♠

(f)   Opener   Responder
      2♡   2♠
      3♡   4♣

In each auction, responder's 2♠ bid showed a hand worth at least 7-8 points with at least ½ quick trick and a five-card or longer spade suit headed by at least the Queen and Jack. His 3♠ bid in auction (e) is a cue-bid probably showing the spade Ace, since opener's 3♡ rebid set the trump suit. Similarly, responder's 4♣ in auction (f) is a cue-bid in support of hearts. Responder might have:

(e)   ♠ AJxxx   ♡ Jxx   ◇ Kx   ♣ xxx   or

(f)   ♠ Kxxxx   ♡ xxx   ◇ xxx   ♣ Ax

Any change of suit by opener shows a second suit that is probably five cards long.

Responder must continue to bid—and should bid naturally—either supporting opener's first or second suit, or rebidding his own suit if it is a very good one, or bidding NT, or showing a second suit of his own.

Examples—In the auction:

Opener	Responder
2♡	2♠
3♣	

(g)   ♠ A J x x x   ♡ x x   ◇ x x x   ♣ Q x x

Responder should bid 3♡

(h)   ♠ Q J x x x   ♡ x   ◇ x x x   ♣ A x x x

Responder should bid 4♣.

(i)   ♠ K J x x x   ♡ x x   ◇ A J 10 x   ♣ x x

Responder should bid 3 NT. Since opener likely has, at most, a total of three cards in spades and diamonds, responder should have these two suits well stopped in order to bid 3 NT.

(j)   ♠ K Q 10 x x x   ♡ x   ◇ x x x   ♣ K x x

Responder should rebid 3♠.

(k)   ♠ K Q 10 x x   ♡ x   ◇ K x x x x   ♣ x x

Responder should bid 3◇.

Pre-emptive Opening Bids

OPENING BIDS OF 3 OR 4
OF ANY SUIT, OR OF 5 OF A MINOR

Opening bids of three or four of any suit or five of a minor suit are pre-emptive bids and show little high card strength. These bids are intended principally to hinder the opponents rather than to suggest that game may be made.

The pre-empt should be made in a suit of seven or more cards.

The pre-emptive opening normally shows less than the minimum high-card and quick trick strength needed for an opeing one-bid. Opening bids at the three level are usually made with less than 9 or 10 high card points.

Such high card strength as there is should be mostly in the long suit.

While the pre-empter expects to be set, his playing strength should protect him from disaster if he follows the "Rule of Two and Three."

THE RULE OF TWO AND THREE

Because the pre-empter has little high card strength, he must be prepared to be doubled and set by the opponents.

For safety's sake, therefore, he should have a sufficiently good playing hand that he is unlikely to lose more than 500 points if he is doubled. That is, if his side is vulnerable, he should have in hand only two tricks less than are needed to fulfill the contract. If he is not vulnerable, he should have in hand three tricks less than are needed.

Examples:

(a)   ♠ x x   ♡ K Q J x x x x   ◊ x x x   ♣ x

Has prospects for taking six tricks with hearts as trumps. Non-vulnerable, this hand should be opened with 3♡. It is not, however, good enough for a vulnerable 3♡ bid since it is three tricks shy of nine, and a vulnerable three-trick set costs 800 points. If the hand contained one more small heart, a vulnerable 3♡ bid or non-vulnerable 4♡ bid would be called for.

(b)   ♠ A Q J x x x x   ♡ —   ◊ K x   ♣ x x x

This hand presents the other end of the scale. It is a sound vulnerable 4♠ opening, but is too strong for a non- vulnerable 4♠ opening unless partner has already passed. In first or second seat non-vulnerable, therefore, this hand should be opened 1♠.

(c)   ♠ K Q x   ♡ K x x   ◊ 10 x x x x x   ♣ —

Should not be opened with a pre-empt. All of the high cards are in short suits. This hand can be useful to partner if played in a major suit and could be a disaster played in diamonds. Therefore, the hand should be passed.

(d)   ♠ K Q x x   ♡ x   ◊ x   ♣ Q J 10 x x x x

Should not be opened with a pre-empt. The hand does not rate to be a disaster played in clubs, but if 3♣ is opened, a laydown spade game could easily be missed. The hand should be passed initially.

(e)   ♠ x x   ♡ x   ◊ A K Q J x x x x   ♣ x x

This hand has enough playing strength for an opening pre-empt of 4◊ vulnerable or 5◊ non-vulnerable. It would be desirable to pre-empt if the opponents hold the great bulk of the high card strength; but if partner has an average hand (e.g.,   ♠ A x x   ♡ Q J x x x   ◊ x   ♣ Q J x x) 3 NT can likely be made. If partner has not already passed, or if partner and both opponents have passed, the hand should thus be opened with 1◊. Otherwise, it is better to open 4◊ or 5◊ (according to the vulnerability).

RESPONDING TO PRE-EMPTS

After partner has opened with a pre-empt, responder should bear in mind the Rule of Two and Three. Non-vulnerable, responder needs to be able to provide three tricks just for opener to be able to make his bid.

RAISES OF A PRE-EMPTIVE OPENING

Facing a non-vulnerable pre-empt, four or more tricks must be provided if responder is to raise in an attempt to make game or slam. Facing a vulnerable pre-empt, three or more tricks must be provided for game or slam. For example, with a hand such as:

(a)   ♠ A Q x x   ♡ x x   ◇ A x x x   ♣ K J x

facing a non-vulnerable 3♡ pre-empt, responder should pass.

Nevertheless, over a three-level pre-empt, if responder has a very weak hand with a fit for opener's suit, he should often raise—not in an attempt to make game, but in an attempt to increase the pre-empt, making it even harder for the opponents to bid. Thus the auction:

North	East	South	West
3♠	Pass	4♠	

is ambiguous to everyone except South, since South could hold either

(b)   ♠ K x x x   ♡ x x x   ◇ x   ♣ Q x x x x

or (c)   ♠ K x x   ♡ A Q x x   ◇ x x   ♣ A K x x

A raise by responder to the five level after a major suit pre-empt is a slam try asking opener to bid a small slam if he has two of the top three honors in his suit.

Opposite a 3♡ opening, for example, responder would jump to 5♡ with a hand such as:

(d)   ♠ A x x   ♡ J x   ◇ A K Q x x   ♣ A K x

CHANGE OF SUIT BY RESPONDER
OVER A PRE-EMPTIVE OPENING

A change of suit by responder over a three level pre-empt is forcing if the response is not itself a game bid.

If the response is in a major suit at the three level, it is usually a long suit that responder may want to play in if opener has a fit.

If the response is in a minor suit, it is more likely an advance cue-bid in support of opener's long suit—a mild slam try.

Examples:

   (a)   ♠ K Q 10 x x x   ♡ A J x   ◊ A K   ♣ x x

Opposite a 3♣ opening, responder bids 3♠ hoping to catch the pre-empter with at least two spades, with which opener would raise to 4♠.

   (b)   ♠ A J x   ♡ x x x   ◊ A K Q x x   ♣ A x

Facing a 3♠ opening bid, responder bids 4♣ as a cue-bid. Over the probable 4♠ rebid by opener, responder will then cue-bid 5◊ in an effort to coax a 5♡ cue-bid out of the pre-empter if he has a singleton heart.

After a pre-empt of 4♣ or 4◊, a response of 4♡ or 4♠ is not forcing. It is an attempt by responder to play the hand in game in his own long suit.

A change of suit by responder over a pre-empt of four of a major suit or five of a minor suit is a cue-bid in search of slam and is forcing.

3 NOTRUMP RESPONSE TO A PRE-EMPTIVE OPENING

Opposite a three level pre-empt, responder should not bid 3 NT unless he has a fit with opener's suit, stoppers in the unbid major suit or suits, and real prospects of achieving nine tricks.

Examples:

   (a)   ♠ K Q x   ♡ A Q x x   ◊ x x   ♣ K J x x

Opposite a 3◇ opening, responder should pass, since he is unlikely to be able to take many tricks with opener's hand, and thus is not likely to come to nine tricks.

(b)   ♠ K Q x   ♡ A Q x   ◇ K x x   ♣ Q x x x

The presence of the diamond king offers prospects of being able to develop six or seven tricks from his partner's hand. Bid 3 NT.

REBIDS BY THE PRE-EMPTER

Having made his pre-empt, *opener should not bid again unless forced to do so by opener.*

If opener has made his pre-empt according to the Rule of Two and Three, he has described his hand adequately to his partner, and all further actions should be left to responder. Thus, if the auction proceeds:

North	East	South	West
3◇	3 NT	Pass	Pass

North should pass.

After a new suit response over a pre-emptive opening, opener is forced to bid if the response itself was not a bid that constitutes game.

If the pre-empt was at the three level and the response was three of a major suit, opener should raise to four of responder's suit with a doubleton or better in the suit. With a singleton in responder's suit and a good hand for his pre-empt, opener should bid 3 NT. With a poor hand, opener should simply rebid four of his suit.

Examples—After a 3♣ opening and a 3♠ response:

(a)   ♠ x x   ♡ x   ◊ x x x   ♣ K Q J x x x x

Opener should raise to 4♠

(b)   ♠ x   ♡ Q x   ◊ x x x   ♣ A Q J x x x x

Opener should bid 3 NT.

(c)   ♠ x   ♡ x x   ◊ J x x   ♣ K Q 10 x x x x

Opener should bid 4♣.

If over a three or four level pre-empt, responder has made a cue-bid, (for example, by bidding four of a minor suit over a three-level pre-empt or by bidding any new suit at the five level over a 4♡ or 4♠ or higher pre-empt), opener should strain to cue-bid in return, especially if he has a reasonable suit and does not have to bypass game to cue-bid. Such a cue-bid by opener shows an Ace, a King, a void, or a singleton. The singleton is the most frequent cue-biddable value in a pre-empter's hand.

Opening above
the Game Level

OPENINGS OF 5 OR 6 OF A MAJOR;
OPENINGS OF 6 OF A MINOR

Openings at the six or seven level show very powerful hands, promising slam on their own. Similarly, openings of 5♡ or 5♠ show very strong hands, promising eleven tricks. In each case, opener usually has at least one void, and the only tricks he expects to lose are in trumps.

Responder should raise opener's suit, if he has the Ace or King of trumps. He should not become ambitious on the basis of any other Ace or King in his hand.

Examples:

(a)　♠ —　　♡ Q J 10 x x x x x　　◇ A K　　♣ A K Q

Opener should open 5♡.

(b)　♠ A K Q x　　♡ x x　　◇ Q x x x　　♣ J x x

Opposite an opening bid of 5♡, this hand must pass.

183

Opening with
a Part-Score

When the partnership has bid and made any contract that scores less than the 100 points needed for game, it has traveled part of the way toward its goal, for it can build on the points already earned to score the 100-point total needed for game. This headstart toward game is called a part-score or partial; its existence may affect the meanings of many bids of the partnership that owns it.

If the partnership has a partial of less than 60 points, the partial should generally be ignored in deciding whether or not, and if so, with what, to open the bidding.

With a part-score of 60 or more, special attention should be paid to such factors as strength and suit textures.

EFFECT OF PARTIAL ON
FORCING NATURE OF CERTAIN BIDS

The principal effect of the existence of a part-score is that many bids that would be forcing if the slate were clear are not forcing in some circumstances.

In general, any bid, other than a jump shift, that would be forcing without a part-score is *not* forcing *if* the bid would score enough points to complete the game.

184

A jump shift, however, is always forcing (by an unpassed hand) for one round, regardless of the existence or amount of any part-score; it is the only bid that is always forcing with a part-score.

Examples:

(a)   (with a 60-point partial)   *Opener*   *Responder*
                                    1♠   2♣

Responder's 2♣ bid is not forcing because the 40 points to be earned by making 2♣ are all that are needed for game.

(b)   (with a 40-point partial)   *Opener*   *Responder*
                                    1♠   2♣

Responder's 2♣ bid is forcing, just as it would be without a part-score, because the 40 points are not enough to complete the game.

(c)   (with a 60-point partial)   *Opener*   *Responder*
                                    1♠   3♣

(d)   (with a 20-point partial)   *Opener*   *Responder*
                                    1♡   1♠
                                    3♦

The jump shifts by responder and opener, respectively, are forcing for one round, regardless of the amount of the part-score.

With one exception, any bid that is one more than the level of that denomination that is needed to complete the game is a slam try. The one exception is for a raise of opener's suit to the two level. This raise should be used pre-emptively to make it difficult for the opponents to intervene.

Example—In the auction:

(e)   *Opener*   *Responder*
      1♠   3♠

With a 60 point partial, responder's jump to 3♠, while it is not forcing, is a clear slam try since a raise to 2♠ would have sufficed for game.

EFFECT OF PARTIAL OF 60 OR MORE ON STRENGTHS OF CERTAIN OPENINGS

With a partial of 60 or more, a player should strain to open the bidding, even on marginal hands that he would ordinarily pass.

In addition, a player should avoid opening a three-card suit or a suit that is weak. With a partial, there is usually less exploration to find the best demonination in which to play.

With such a partial, the range of the 1 NT opening bid is enlarged by about a point in each direction to 15-19 high card points; the range of the 2 NT opening becomes 21-24 high card points. In part, the goal of these enlargements is to avoid the need to open a weak suit; and in part, the goal is to make it more difficult for the opponents to compete effectively to prevent a game-going declaration.

Examples—With a partial of 60:

(a)   ♠ A K J x   ♡ K J x   ◇ x x x   ♣ J x x

This hand, with a part-score, should be opened 1♠, even though without a part-score it could be passed because of rebid problems.

(b)   ♠ K x   ♡ A x x   ◊ K Q x   ♣ Q x x x x

Best opened with 1 NT with a partial; that opening makes it far more difficult for the opponents to intervene than if the hand were opened with 1♣.

(c)   ♠ K Q x   ♡ A Q x x   ◊ Q x x x   ♣ A Q

This hand should be opened 1 NT.

SHADED VALUES FOR FORCING TWO-BIDS

"Forcing" two-bids may be made on shaded values in order to avoid opener's having to rebid at the three level. Strong two-bids are no longer absolutely forcing if the bid would be enough to complete the game. Even so, responder will normally keep the bidding open unless he has a complete bust.

Example—With a partial of 60:

(a)   ♠ A K Q x x x   ♡ A x x   ◊ x x   ♣ x

This hand should be opened 2♠.

RESPONSE TO OPENINGS WHEN THERE IS A PARTIAL

Because responder, too, will strain to reach a contract that will bring enough points to complete the game and because he will wish to avoid getting overboard unnecessarily, the ranges of most of the standard minimum responses are expanded:

A 1 NT response promises 4-12 points.

A jump to 2 NT shows 13-16 points.

A non-jump raise of opener's suit promises 6-12 points.

A jump raise of opener's suit shows 13-16 points.

A new suit response (even at the two level if the bid suffices for game) shows 6-16 points.

Examples:

(a)   ♠ x x   ♡ K x x x   ◇ x x   ♣ x x x x x

(b)   ♠ A x   ♡ K J x x   ◇ K x x   ♣ x x x x

With a 60 point partial, responder should raise opener's 1♡ bid to 2♡ with both of the above hands.

OPENING AGAINST A PARTIAL HELD BY OPPONENTS

If the opponents have a part-score, it is important to strain to open the bidding before one of them can do so. The chief goal of opening lightly when the opponents have a partial is to inhibit their quest for a cheap game; and in part, the goal is to avoid the danger of having to overcall or balance when the opponents may have extra values for their bids.

When the opponents have a part-score, therefore, it is advisable to open the bidding with any reasonable 12-point hand.

Slam Bidding

The foundation for good slam bidding is a sound understanding of the early rounds of the bidding—a sense of which bids show extra strength and which show only modest values. Good slam bidding requires the ability to visualize accurately the usefulness of long suits, and the existence of fits and controls.

After the partnership has determined that it probably has enough strength and/or length to win 12 tricks, it may need to doublecheck to be sure that the opponents cannot take two tricks to defeat the slam.

The principal tools are cue-bids to be sure that the partnership will not lose the first two tricks in a side suit, the Blackwood and Gerber conventions to be sure that the partnership is not missing two Aces, and trump quality asking bids, such as the Grand Slam Force, to be sure that the trump suit is sufficiently solid.

CUE-BIDS

A cue-bid is a forcing bid in a suit that the bidder cannot want to be the trump suit. The bid of a suit that has been bid naturally by the opponents is a cue-bid.

When the partnership is committed to game and a suit has been

189

agreed upon, either explicitly or implicitly, a bid in a new suit is a cue-bid.

This cue-bid is an invitation to slam.

Examples:

    (a)   *Opener*   *Responder*
               1♠   3♠
               4♣

Spades have been explicitly agreed as trumps. Opener's 4♣ bid is a cue-bid in search of slam.

    (b)   *Opener*   *Responder*
             1 NT   3♠
               4♦

Spades have been implicitly agreed as trumps since opener may not introduce a new suit in which he wants to play after having opened 1 NT. Thus, his 4♦ bid is a cue-bid that confirms agreement on spades as trumps and expresses an interest in slam.

    (c)   *Opener*   *Responder*
               1♥   2♥
               3♣

Opener's bid of 3♣ is not a slam-going cue-bid even though hearts have been agreed as trumps. His 3♣ bid is simply a game try, showing 17 or more points.

WHAT THE CUE-BID SHOWS

A cue-bid shows control of the suit bid. First-round control of a suit consists of the Ace or a void. Second-round control consists of the King or a singleton.

The first cue-bid in an auction normally shows first-round control.

When cue-bidding it is customary to make the cheapest possible cue-bid. If a player makes a cue-bid in other than the cheapest suit, he denies having the Ace in any suit he has bypassed.

Example:

   (a)   *Opener*   *Responder*
        1♠   3♠
        4◊

The 4◊ cue-bid promises the Ace or a void in diamonds, but denies such a holding in clubs.

After the first cue-bid, further cue-bids may show first-round or second-round control of the suits cue-bid. If the further cue-bid is in a suit in which the cue-bidder has denied a first round control (by bypassing that suit in order to make his first cue-bid), he shows the King or a singleton in the suit of the later cue-bid.

Example:

   (b)   *Opener*   *Responder*
        1♠   3♠
        4◊   4♡
        5♣   5◊

Opener's 4◊ bid shows the Ace or a void in diamonds. Responder's 4♡ cue-bid normally promises the Ace or a void in hearts. Opener's 5♣ cue-bid shows only the King or a singleton in clubs. If opener had first round control of clubs, his bid over the raise to 3♠ would have been 4♣ rather than

4◇. Responder's further cue-bid of 5◇ shows second-round control of diamonds. With first-round control, responder would not cue-bid in diamonds since his partner has already shown first-round control of that suit. Responder's cue-bid of a second-round diamond control suggests that he probably has no additional first-round controls to show.

RESPONDING TO CUE-BIDS

A player whose partner has made a cue-bid should assess the strength of his hand in light of his partner's slam invitation.

He has three options: he can return to the agreed trump suit if his hand is completely unsuitable for slam; or he can jump to slam if the cue-bid gives him all the information he needs to make slam a reasonable proposition; or with a hand that fits into neither of these categories, he can cue-bid in return.

Examples—If the auction has begun:

Opener	Responder
1♠	3♠
4♣	

(a)   ♠ Q x x x   ♡ x x   ◇ K Q x   ♣ A J x x

Responder should bid 4♠, since his hand is unsuited to slam opposite the club void suggested by opener's cue-bid.

(b)   ♠ Q x x x   ♡ A K x x   ◇ x x   ♣ K x x

Responder should cue-bid 4♡ since he has an interest in slam, but has no assurance that there are not two quick diamond losers.

(c)   ♠ K x x x x x   ♡ —   ◊ A K x x   ♣ x x x

Responder may jump to 6♠. Alternatively, he may cue-bid 4◊ to hear what opener does next. However, he is unlikely to be able to determine that opener has enough quick club and heart winners to take care of all of responder's little clubs and that opener has either the queen or a doubleton in diamonds, all of which information is needed before a grand slam could be bid with certainty.

If the opening bid has been a non-vulnerable pre-empt of 3♡, and responder has cue-bid 4♣, and the opener holds:

(d)   ♠ x x   ♡ A Q J x x x x   ◊ x   ♣ Q x x

Opener should rebid 4◊, cue-bidding his singleton. He should not be concerned at this stage with his small doubleton in spades, because responder's bypass of spades to cue-bid 4♣ does not deny the Ace of spades, for the simple reason that the response of 3♠ to the opening 3♡ bid would not be a cue-bid but a natural bid in hopes of playing the hand in spades. Since opener has a very good suit for his pre-empt and can return the cue-bid below the game level, he should do so.

If opener's singleton were in spades and he had a doubleton diamond, he should probably cue-bid 4♠ with such a good heart suit, but decline to go past 4♡ if his suit were worse.

BLACKWOOD

HOW TO SHOW ACES AND KINGS

The Blackwood convention is a 4 NT bid that asks partner how many Aces he has.

The Ace-showing responses are:

$$5\clubsuit = \text{No Aces or 4 Aces}$$
$$5\diamondsuit = 1\text{ Ace}$$
$$5\heartsuit = 2\text{ Aces}$$
$$5\spadesuit = 3\text{ Aces}$$

If the Blackwood bidder rebids 5 NT after any of the Ace- showing responses, *he guarantees that the partnership has all of the Aces*, and asks responder how many Kings he has. The bid of 5 NT asks about Kings *only* if it has been preceded by a 4 NT Blackwood bid. Thus, a player who holds all four Aces must bid 4 NT to ask about Aces first, even knowing his partner has none, in order for his 5 NT bid to ask about Kings.

The King-showing responses are:

$$6\clubsuit \quad = \text{No Kings}$$
$$6\diamondsuit \quad = 1\text{ King}$$
$$6\heartsuit \quad = 2\text{ Kings}$$
$$6\spadesuit \quad = 3\text{ Kings}$$
$$6\,NT = 4\text{ Kings}$$

If the partner of the Blackwood bidder has a long solid suit, he is allowed, over the 5 NT bid asking for Kings, to jump to 7 of his suit instead of automatically showing how many Kings he has.

If after hearing how many Aces his partner has, the Blackwood bidder wants to play the hand not in slam, but in 5 NT, he may bid a new suit at the five level. So long as the suit cannot be taken for the trump suit, the bid asks the Blackwood responder himself to bid 5 NT.

WHEN BLACKWOOD SHOULD NOT BE USED

Blackwood should not be used unless it has been determined that the partnership probably has enough tricks for slam. It is of little importance that the partnership has all the Aces and Kings if it can only take 10 or 11 tricks.

Blackwood should not be used by a player who has a weak doubleton in his hand, for even if the partnership is missing only one Ace, the opponents may be able to cash both the Ace and King of the weak suit.

Blackwood is not the most useful toold for a hand containing a void, for even if the partnership is found to be missing two Aces, slam may be a good prospect if one of the missing Aces is in the void suit of Blackwood bidder.

Blackwood should not be used by a hand containing only one Ace if clubs are the agreed trump suit, for if the response is 5♦, showing only one Ace, the partnership will have bid beyond its makeable five-club game.

For similar reasons, Blackwood should not be used by a hand containing no Aces if diamonds are to be trumps, for the two-Ace showing response of 5♥ will get the partnership too high.

WHEN A 4 NOTRUMP BID IS BLACKWOOD

It is sometimes difficult to know whether or not a 4 NT bid is Blackwood at all, rather than another type of slam try, or a takeout bid, or an attempt to play the hand in 4 NT. Here are the guidelines:

If a trump suit has specifically been agreed upon, 4 NT is Blackwood.

Example—In the auction:

   (a)   *Opener*   *Responder*
          1♠   4♠
          4 NT

The 4 NT bid is Blackwood.

If 4 NT has been bid as a jump over a bid in a suit, it is Blackwood.

Example:

   (b)   *Opener*   *Responder*
          1♡   2♣
          3♡   4 NT

The 4 NT bid is Blackwood.

If 4 NT has been bid by a player who has opened with a forcing two-bid or by a responder whose first bid was a jump shift, 4 NT is Blackwood.

Examples:

   (c)   *Opener*   *Responder*
          2♠   2 NT
          4 NT

   (d)   *Opener*   *Responder*
          1♡   3♢
          3 NT   4 NT

In the above two auctions, the 4 NT bids are Blackwood.

If 4 NT is bid by a player who has jumped to three of a suit over a 1 NT opening, and opener has raised the suit either directly or inferentially (by cue-bidding), the 4 NT bid is Blackwood.

Example:

(e)   *Opener   Responder*
    1 NT   3♡
    4♣   4 NT

Responder's 4 NT bid is Blackwood.

If, however, over a 1 NT opening responder has jumped to three of a suit and opener has merely rebid 3 NT, responder's bid of 4 NT is ambiguous.

Example:

(f)   *Opener   Responder*
    1 NT   3♡
    3 NT   4 NT

Some partnerships consider that responder's 4 NT bid is quantitative, asking opener to bid a slam with a maximum point count. Others, realizing that responder has no other way to show his suit and then ask about Aces, consider the 4 NT bid to be Blackwood. Without any specific understanding, it is best to treat this 4 NT bid as Blackwood.

If 4 NT is bid by a player at his first genuine opportunity to do so over a suit bid, or at his first opportunity after he and his partner have cue-bid, it is Blackwood.

Examples:

(g)   *Opener*   *Responder*
       4♡   4 NT

(h)   *Opener*   *Responder*
       1♠   3♠
       4♣   4◊
       4 NT

The 4 NT bids are Blackwood.

WHEN A 4 NOTRUMP BID IS NOT BLACKWOOD

If the opening bid has been in NT and no suit has been bid naturally, a 4 NT bid is not Blackwood. It is instead a quantitative bid asking opener to bid 6 NT with a maximum point count.

Example:

(a)   *Opener*   *Responder*
       1 NT   2♣
       2◊   4 NT

No suit has been bid naturally, 2♣ being Stayman. The 2◊ rebid merely denies a four-card major suit. The 4 NT bid is thus quantitative rather than Blackwood. Responder might have a hand such as:

♠ K Q x x   ♡ A x   ◊ Q J x   ♣ A x x x

If the bid immediately preceding the 4 NT bid was in NT and has a specific point range, and if the 4 NT bidder has not jump shifted or opened with a forcing two-bid, 4 NT is usually not Blackwood—it is quantitative.

Examples:

(b)	Opener	Responder	(c)	Opener	Responder
	1♣	1♡		1♠	2 NT
	2 NT	4 NT		4 NT	

(d)	Opener	Responder
	1♠	2♢
	3 NT	4 NT

In auctions (b), (c), and (d), the 4 NT bids are quantitative—not Ace-asking Blackwood.

If the auction is one in which a 4♣ bid by the 4 NT bidder would have been the Gerber convention, 4 NT is not Blackwood. Instead, in such an auction, 4 NT is quantitative, asking that slam be bid with a maximum point count for the previous bidding.

Examples:

(e)	Opener	Responder
	1 NT	2♣
	2♡	4 NT

A 4♣ bid by responder at his second turn would have been Gerber, asking about Aces; thus his 4 NT bid is not Blackwood.

(f)	Opener	Responder
	1♡	3♡
	3 NT	4 NT

4♣ by responder at his second turn would not have been Gerber; thus his 4 NT bid is Blackwood.

If neither partner has supported the other's suit and the bidding has already reached the four level without there having been an opening two-bid or jump shift by the 4 NT bidder, a 4 NT bid is not Blackwood, but is an attempt to play the hand in 4 NT.

Examples:

(g)	*Opener*	*Responder*	(h)	*Opener*	*Responder*
	1♠	2◇		2♡	3◇
	2♡	4◇		4♣	4 NT
	4 NT				

In auctions (g) and (h), the 4 NT bid is simply a suggestion that the hand be played in NT.

If the 4 NT bidder has shown a willingness to play the hand in game without encouraging a move toward slam, his 4 NT bid is not Blackwood.

Examples:

(i)	*Opener*	*Responder*
	1♠	3◇
	3 NT	4♣
	4 NT	

(j)	*North*	*East*	*South*	*West*
	1♡	1♠	3♡	3♠
	4♡	Pass	Pass	4♠
	4 NT			

In auctions (i) and (j), the 4 NT bids are not Blackwood. In each instance, the bid represents an attempt to play the hand in 4 NT.

If 4 NT has been bid over an opponent's opening pre-empt of 4♡ or 4♠, it is not Blackwood, but instead is a takeout bid. The meaning of a 4 NT bid over an opponent's opening pre-empt of 4♣ or 4◇ is a subject for discussion; some partnerships treat it as an attempt to play in 4 NT and some treat it as Blackwood. The meaning of this bid has not been standardized.

RESPONDING TO BLACKWOOD WITH A VOID

If one member of the partnership is void in a side suit, a slam may be makeable even if the Ace of that suit is missing.

There are special responses to a Blackwood 4 NT bid to show a void, but first it should be recognized that in some circumstances a void should not be shown at all.

The partner of the Blackwood bidder should not show a void if to do so would get the partnership too high. If he has no Aces at all, the Blackwood responder usually should not bother to show a void. In addition, if the partner of the Blackwood bidder has a void, he should not show it unless he considers it to be a useful void—in other words, not a void in one of his partner's suits. A void in an unbid suit or in the opponent's suit is generally considered to be a feature worth showing.

The most common method of showing a void is to jump to the six level over 4 NT, to the suit that would have been bid on the five level to show the number of Aces held.

$$6◇ = 1 \text{ Ace and a void}$$
$$6♡ = 2 \text{ Aces and a void}$$
$$6♠ = 3 \text{ Aces and a void}$$

This method does not identify for the Blackwood bidder the precise location of his partner's void, but he does know that the void is considered to be in a "useful" suit.

COPING WITH AN OPPONENT'S INTERFERENCE OVER BLACKWOOD

If an opponent overcalls over the 4 NT Blackwood bid, the standard method for defending is to double with any hand on which the penalty appears likely to exceed the points to be earned in the most likely makeable contract. If the penalty does not appear to be sufficiently high, the Blackwood responder should pass with no Aces, and bid the next higher suit over the overcall to show one Ace, two suits higher to show two Aces, and so forth.

GERBER

The Gerber convention is a 4♣ bid that asks partner how many Aces he has. The Ace-showing responses are:

$$
\begin{array}{ll}
4\diamondsuit & = \text{No Aces or 4 Aces} \\
4\heartsuit & = 1 \text{ Ace} \\
4\spadesuit & = 2 \text{ Aces} \\
4\,\text{NT} & = 3 \text{ Aces}
\end{array}
$$

If the four club bidder bids 5♣ over the Ace-showing response, he asks his partner how many Kings he has. The King showing responses are:

$$
\begin{array}{ll}
5\diamondsuit & = \text{No Kings} \\
5\heartsuit & = 1 \text{ King} \\
5\spadesuit & = 2 \text{ Kings} \\
5\,\text{NT} & = 3 \text{ Kings} \\
6\clubsuit & = 4 \text{ Kings}
\end{array}
$$

WHEN IS A 4♣ BID GERBER?

Most experts use a 4♣ bid as Gerber only after NT has been opened, responded or rebid by the partner of the four club bidder.

Examples:

	(a)	Opener	Responder	(b)	Opener	Responder
		1 NT	4♣		2 NT	4♣

	(c)	Opener	Responder	(d)	Opener	Responder
		1♡	1♠		1♠	2 NT
		2 NT	4♣		4♣	

	(e)	Opener	Responder
		1 NT	2♣
		2♠	4♣

In each of the above auctions, the four club bid is Gerber.

It is not recommended to use the 4♣ bid as Gerber in suit oriented auctions because 4♣ is often more useful as a cue-bid than as an Ace-asking bid.

Examples:

	(f)	Opener	Responder	(g)	Opener	Responder
		1♠	3♠		1 NT	3♠
		4♣			4♣	

In the above two auctions, the 4♣ bid should be used to show first-round control of clubs.

GERBER AFTER A 3 NOTRUMP OPENING

After a 3 NT opening, there are two possible uses for a 4♣ response. One is the Stayman convention to determine whether or not the opener has a four-card major suit. The other is the Gerber convention to ask how many Aces opener has.

Since a 4◊ bid can be used to ask about major suits with little loss of information, a 4♣ response to 3 NT should be used as Gerber.

GRAND SLAM FORCE

The Grand Slam Force is a device to ensure that the trump suit is solid when the partnership is considering bidding a grand slam. It consists of a jump to 5 NT either after a trump suit has been agreed upon, or inferentially agreeing to a trump suit by the jump.

The 5 NT bid asks partner to bid a grand slam if he has two of the top three honors in the trump suit: the Ace and King, or the Ace and Queen, or the King and Queen.

Examples:

(a)   *Opener   Responder*
        1♠   3♠
        5 NT

Opener's 5 NT bid asks responder to bid 7♠ with two of the top three spade honors.

(b)   *Opener   Responder*
        1♡   5 NT

The jump to 5 NT inferentially agrees on hearts as trumps and asks opener to bid 7♡ with two of the top three heart honors.

The jump to 5 NT is forcing since if the partner of the 5 NT bidder lacks two of the top three trump honors, he must return to six of the agreed suit.

Since six is the lowest level at which the partnership can stop, the 5 NT bidder should have a trump holding that will be adequate to make a small slam if his partner has none of the top three trump honors.

Examples:

(c)   ♠ A K x   ♡ Q x x x   ◇ —   ♣ A K Q x x x

Opposite a 1♡ opening, the Grand Slam Force is inappropriate. If opener has neither the Ace nor the King of hearts, the partnership will not be safe at the six level.

(d)   ♠ A x   ♡ x x x x x x   ◇ A K Q J x   ♣ —

The Grand Slam Force is inappropriate opposite a 1♡ opening because the grand slam may not be makeable even if opener has two of the top three trump honors: he may have the King and Queen.

The Grand Slam Force should not be used if the partnership has a probable loser outside the trump suit. Its only use is to determine trump suit quality.

Example:

(e)   ♠ A x x x   ♡ x   ◊ x   ♣ A K Q J x x x

Opposite a 1♠ opening, the Grand Slam Force is inappropriate until responder determines whether opener has the Aces of hearts and diamonds.

GRAND SLAM FORCE AFTER BLACKWOOD

After Blackwood has been used, 5 NT cannot be used as the Grand Slam Force. Some partnerships agree that unless clubs is the agreed trump suit, a bid of 6♣ over the Blackwood response is the Grand Slam Force.

Example:

(a)   Opener   Responder
　　　　 1♠　　　　 3♠
　　　　 4 NT　　　 5◊
　　　　 6♣

In this auction, spades is the agreed trump suit; 4 NT is Blackwood, and 5◊ shows one Ace. 6♣ is the Grand Slam Force, asking responder to bid 7♠ with two of the top three spade honors. Opener might have a hand such as:

♠ A x x x x x   ♡ A K Q x x   ◊ x   ♣ A

With such a hand, a 5 NT bid asking for Kings would not suffice unless responder had three Kings, since if he had only one or two, the King of trumps might be missing.

VOLUNTARY BID OF FIVE OF THE AGREED MAJOR SUIT

When a major suit has been agreed on and the opponents have not forced the bidding to the five level, the voluntary bid of five of the agreed major trump suit asks partner to bid a small slam with a particular holding in a particular suit.

The precise suit in question depends on the previous auction. It may be the trump suit, or a suit bid by the opponents, or a suit that has not been bid at all.

INVITATION TO BID SLAM WITH TWO OF THE TOP THREE TRUMP HONORS

If the 5♡ or 5♠ bid is made in an auction in which two or three suits have not been mentioned by the declaring side, the bid asks partner, with one exception, to bid a small slam with two of the top three trump honors.

Examples:

(a) *Opener*   *Responder*   (b) *Opener*   *Responder*
    1♠   3♠   1♠   3♠
    5♠   4♣   5♠

In each auction, the five spade bid asks the other member of the partnership to bid 6♠ if his spade holding includes the Ace-King, the King-Queen, or the Ace-Queen. Opener's hand in (a) might be:

     ♠ J x x x x   ♡ A K Q 10 x   ◇ A x x   ♣ —

Responder's hand in (b) might be:

     ♠ x x x x x x   ♡ A K x x   ◇ —   ♣ K J x

The exception occurs when the partner of the player who has bid five of the agreed major suit has shown a very weak hand, as by raising an opening bid to the two level. Since such a responder rarely will have two of the top three trump honors, opener's bid of five of the agreed major suit will ask such a responder to bid slam with *one* of the top three trump honors.

Example:

(c)   *Opener   Responder*
    1♡   2♡
    5♡

Opener might have a hand such as:

    ♠ —   ♡ Q x x x x x x   ◇ A K J x x   ♣ A

INVITATION TO BID SLAM WITH FIRST OR SECOND ROUND CONTROL OF THE ONLY UNBID SUIT

If there is only one unbid suit at the time of the bid of five of the agreed major suit, the bid asks partner to bid a small slam with either the Ace, or the King, or a singleton or a void in the unbid suit.

Example:

(a)   *Opener   Responder*
    1♡   3♡
    3♠   4♣
    5♡

Opener's 5♡ bid asks responder to bid 6♡ with second round control of diamonds. His hand might be:

    ♠ A Q   ♡ A K x x x x   ◇ x x   ♣ K x x

INVITATION TO BID SLAM WITH FIRST OR
SECOND ROUND CONTROL OF THE OPPONENT'S SUIT

If the bid of 5♡ or 5♠ occurs in an auction in which an opponent has bid a suit, the bid asks that a slam be bid with at least second round control of the opponent's suit, *unless* the 5♡ or 5♠ bid has been preceded by a cue-bid of the opponent's suit.

Example:

(a)	North	East	South	West
	1♡	1♠	2♢	3♠
	4♡	Pass	5♡	

South's 5♡ bid asks North to bid 6♡ if he has first or second round control of spades, the opponent's suit. The 5♡ bid would have had the same meaning if South had bid it directly over East's 1♠ overcall.

If there has been a cue-bid of the opponent's suit, the 5♡ or 5♠ bid retains the meaning it would have had if there had been no bid by the opponent.

Examples:

(b)	North	East	South	West
	1♡	1♠	2♢	Pass
	2♡	Pass	2♠	Pass
	3♡	Pass	5♡	

South's 5♡ bid after the cue-bid of spades asks North to bid 6♡ with first or second round control of the only suit his side has not bid, i.e., clubs.

(c) | North | East | South | West |
|------|------|-------|------|
| 1♡ | 1♠ | 2♠ | Pass |
| 3♡ | Pass | 5♡ | |

There are two suits that North-South have not bid. Thus, South's 5♡ bid asks North to bid 5♡ if he has two of the top three heart honors.

Notrump Overcalls

After an opponent has opened the bidding, a player who enters the auction must have appropriate strength and distribution to avoid suffering a costly penalty at the hands of the opponents. At the same time, he tries to describe his hand sufficently for his partner to assess his side's prospects.

Overcalls in notrump are the most precise—and the most dangerous—means of entering the auction.

STRENGTH REQUIRED FOR A NON-JUMP NOTRUMP OVERCALL

The strength required to bid NT after one or both of the opponents have bid increases with the level of the opponents' bids.

ONE NOTRUMP OVERCALL

A 1 NT overcall is a bid of 1 NT after righthand opponent has bid or after both opponents have bid. Its meaning is essentially the same in both cases.

A 1 NT overcall promises 16-19 high card points.* With less than

*A NT bid after only the lefthand opponent has bid is a "balancing" bid and promises considerably less strength. (See page 270.)

16 points, a player should either overcall in a suit if his hand contains a suit that is long and strong enough, or make a takeout double if his hand is suited for that call, or pass.

With more than 19 points a player should make a takeout double and then rebid in NT (assuming his hand meets the other requirements for NT bidding). With 20-21 points, his rebid should be the cheapest possible number of NT. With 22-23 points, his rebid should be a single jump in NT.

NON-JUMP OVERCALLS OF 2 NOTRUMP

A non-jump overcall of 2 NT after an opponent's opening bid in a suit requires a minimum of 16 high card points if only the righthand opponent has bid.

If both opponents have bid, making it likely that partner has only 1 or 2 points, a player should have at least 17 points and a reasonable suit to provide him with playing tricks.

Holding the requisite number of points but lacking the playing strength, a takeout double should be used instead of a NT overcall.

If the opponent has opened with 1 NT, an "overcall" of 2 NT is essentially a cue-bid, showing a strong, two-suited hand, rather than a balanced hand. Any combination of two suits is possible.

Example:

   (a)   ♠ x   ♡ K Q x x x x   ◇ x   ♣ A K Q x x

This hand would overcall 2 NT over a 1 NT opening. The overcaller's partner is required to bid over 2 NT.

NON-JUMP OVERCALL OF 3 NOTRUMP

An overcall of 3 NT over a three-level opening promises at least 18 high card points.

If the NT overcall was made over a response at the three level, the hand should also contain a suit with a good source of playing tricks.

NON-JUMP OVERCALL OF 4 NOTRUMP

The meaning of an overcall of 4 NT over a four-level opening bid depends on what suit was opened.

If the opening bid was 4 ♠, the 4 NT bid is takeout; the doubler may have either a two-suited or a three-suited hand.

If the opening bid was 4 ♡, the 4 NT bid is takeout for the minor suits.

If the opening bid was 4 ♣ or 4 ◊, the meaning of the 4 NT bid is not standardized; it is treated by some partnerships as natural, showing a desire to play in 4 NT, and by others as Blackwood.

DISTRIBUTION REQUIRED
FOR OVERCALLING IN NOTRUMP

To overcall in NT, a player should have a relatively balanced hand. The following distributions are permissible: 4-3-3-3, 4-4-3-2, 5-3-3-2, 5-4-2-2, and 6-3-2-2 if the six-card suit is a minor.

With a five-card suit, the suit should be a minor, or if it is a major suit it should be a very weak one—worse than Q J x x x.

If the opening bid has been in clubs or diamonds, a NT overcall should not be made with a hand that contains two four-card major suits. Holding both major suits, it is better to make a takeout double, asking partner to choose a suit.

If the opening bid has been in hearts or spades, it is usually better not to overcall in NT with four cards in the other major suit. On such a hand, a takeout double should be considered.

STOPPERS REQUIRED
FOR NOTRUMP OVERCALLS

To overcall in NT, a player should have secure stoppers in the suit or suits bid by the opponents. A holding of Q J x is the minimum. In addition, no more than one unbid suit should be unguarded.

With two suits unguarded, a player should not overcall in NT, but should rather overcall in a suit or make a takeout double, or should pass, awaiting further developments.

Examples:

    (a)   ♠ A Q x x   ♡ K x   ◇ A K x x   ♣ Q x x

If the bidding is opened 1♠ by East, South should overcall 1 NT. If the opening bid were 1♡, however, a takeout double would be preferable because South has length in the unbid major suit, only a modest stopper in hearts, and a suit-oriented playing hand.

    (b)   ♠ K Q x   ♡ K Q x   ◇ K Q x   ♣ K Q x x

Although he has adequate stoppers for a NT overcall, South should double over any opening by East. His hand is too strong for an immediate 1 NT overcall after a one-level opening, and does not have a suit that offers enough playing tricks after an opening at the two or three level.

    (c)   ♠ A K Q x   ♡ A Q x   ◇ J x x   ♣ J x x

If East opens with 1♣ or 1◇, South should make a takeout double rather than overcalling 1 NT, since he has no stopper in East's suit. If East instead had opened 1♡, in which South does indeed have a stopper, South still should not

overcall 1 NT, since he has two suits unstopped; it is prefer-
able for South to overcall 1♠ on his four-card suit. And if
the opening is 1♠, East should pass.

RESPONSES BY PARTNER
TO 1 NOTRUMP OVERCALL

Responding to a 1 NT overcall is very similar to responding to a
1 NT opening. It is appropriate in responding to the overcall, however, to be a bit more aggressive, for after an opponent has opened,
the location of most of the missing high cards is known. Game
should be bid if the partnership has 25 or more points.

Bearing in mind that the 1 NT overcall promises 16-19 points,
the overcaller's partner should try for game with 7-8 points and
force to game with 9 or more points.

ENCOURAGING AND DISCOURAGING
RESPONSES TO 1 NOTRUMP OVERCALL

The forcing responses to a 1 NT overcall are:

A cue-bid in the opponent's suit.

A jump to a suit at the three level.

A jump to 4♣, the Gerber convention.

The cue-bid in opener's suit is used as the Stayman convention,
asking whether the overcaller has four cards in an unbid major suit.

**The chief invitational response to a NT overcall is 2 NT, showing
7-8 points.** The cue-bid in opener's suit also may be made with 7-8
points.

Any bid of a new suit at the two level is a sign off, showing a long suit and 0-6 points. A 2♣ response to the 1 NT overcall is a sign off in clubs and not Stayman, *unless* the opening bid was 1♣.

CHOOSING A SUIT AFTER A 1 NOTRUMP OVERCALL

If the partner of the over-caller has a balanced hand without a four-card or longer unbid major suit

He should seek to have the hand played in NT, by passing with 0-6 points, raising to 2 NT with 7-8 points, or jumping to 3 NT with 9 or more points.

If the partner of the over-caller has a balanced hand with four cards in any unbid major suit

He should pass if he has 0-6 points. If he has 7 or more points, he should cue-bid opener's suit.

If the partner of the over-caller has a five-card or longer major suit

He should bid two of his suit if he has 0-6 points. If he has 9 or more points, he should jump to three of his suit with a five-card suit or jump to four of his suit if it contains six or more cards. If he has a six-card or longer suit and hand with which he can envision slam possibilities, he should jump to three of his suit and then bid four of his suit. If he has 7-8 points, he should cue-bid to start a sequence that invites game.

If the partner of the over-caller has an unbalanced hand with a long minor suit and no four-card major

He should seek a final NT contract unless his hand is very weak. With 0-6 points, he should sign off in two of his suit (assuming that it is not the suit of the opening bid). But with 7-8 points, he should raise to 2 NT, and with 9 or more points, he should jump to 3 NT. If he has a six-card or longer suit and a hand with which he can envision slam possibilities, he should jump to three of his suit. This bid is forcing to game.

If the partner of the over-caller has an unbalanced hand with a long minor suit and a four-card major

He should bid 2 of his minor suit with 0-6 points. If he has 7 or more points, he should cue-bid opener's suit.

SECOND BID
BY NOTRUMP OVERCALLER

If the response to the 1 NT overcall was a new suit at the two level

Overcaller should pass unless he has 18-19 points and a good fit (Q x x or better) for his partner's suit. In the latter case, he may raise to three.

If the overcaller's partner jumped to three of a major suit

Overcaller should bid 3 NT with a doubleton in the suit, or raise to game in the suit with three-card or longer support.

If the response was 2 NT

Overcaller should bid 3 NT with 18-19 points. Otherwise, he should pass.

If the response to the 1 NT overcall was a cue-bid of opener's suit

If overcaller has four cards in an unbid major suit, he should bid the suit. Without four cards in an unbid major, he should bid 2 NT with 16-17 points, or 3 NT with 18-19 points.

SECOND BID BY PARTNER OF NOTRUMP OVERCALLER

If the 1 NT overcaller's partner has made a cue-bid response, promising at least 7-8 points and length in an unbid major suit, he should take the following actions over rebids by the NT overcaller.

If overcaller has bid two of the major suit in which his partner has length

Partner of the overcaller should raise to three with 7-8 points, or raise to four with 9 or more points.

If overcaller has bid 2 NT or two of a suit other than a major in which his partner has length	With 7-8 points, the partner of the overcaller should bid the minimum number of his major suit if it contains five or more cards, or bid thee of a minor suit if it contains six or more cards; with other holdings, he should settle for 2 NT. These bids are not forcing, but invite game if the overcaller has a maximum. With 9 or more points, the partner of the overcaller should bid 3 NT.
If overcaller has rebid 3 NT	Partner of the overcaller should pass.

If the NT overcaller's partner has signed off by bidding two of his suit directly over the 1 NT overcall and overcaller has raised the suit, the partner of the overcaller should pass with 0-4 points. With 5-6 points, he should bid a game. If his suit is clubs or diamonds, he should bid 3 NT. If his suit is hearts or spades, he should bid four of his suit.

Examples:

North	East	South	West
1♡	1 NT	Pass	2♡
Pass	2 NT	Pass	3♠

West's series of bids show 7-8 points with a five- or six-card spade suit. He might have a hand such as:

(a)   ♠ A Q x x x   ♡ x x   ◊ x x   ♣ x x x x

East has denied having four spades by his 2 NT rebid, and suggests that he has 16-17 points rather than 18-19 by his bid of 2 NT, rather than 3 NT. He might hold any of the following three hands:

(b)   ♠ K x   ♡ Q J x x   ◊ A K x   ♣ K J x x

Overcaller should pass the 3♠ bid because he has only two spades.

(c)   ♠ K x x   ♡ K Q x x   ◊ K Q J x   ♣ Q J

Overcaller should pass since his values are more suitable for NT play than for suit play.

(d)   ♠ K x x   ♡ K Q x x   ◊ A Q x x   ♣ K x

Overcaller's values are excellent for suit play and he has three-card support for his partner's suit and a ruffing value in clubs. Therefore, overcaller should raise to 4♠. Note that the knowledge that most of the missing high cards are located in the hand to the right of the NT overcaller justifies taking an optimistic view.

STRENGTH REQUIRED FOR A JUMP-OVERCALL IN NOTRUMP

A jump to 2 NT over an opponent's opening bid shows a hand worth 19-20 points with good playing strength.

A perfect hand for a jump to 2 NT over a 1 ◊ opening would be:

♠ K x   ♡ Q x   ◇ A Q x   ♣ A K Q x x x

If an opponent opens a weak two-bid, a jump to 3 NT shows a hand similar to the above hand.

Over a one-level opening, a jump overcall of 3 NT shows a slightly stronger hand with slightly more playing strength.

Example:

♠ A x   ♡ K x   ◇ K x   ♣ A K Q J x x x

RESPONSES TO A JUMP OVERCALL OF 2 NOTRUMP

The partner of the player who has made a jump overcall of 2 NT has several options:

With 0-4 points	He should pass, regardless of his distribution, for any bid he makes is forcing to game.
With 6 points or a good 5, and no singleton	He should raise to 3 NT.
With 5 or more points and a singleton or a good five-card or longer suit	He may bid his suit at the three level. This bid is forcing to game.
With 5-12 points and a good six-card major suit (Q J x x x x or better)	He may bid his suit at the four level. The jump to four of a major suit is not a slam try.

Examples—Facing a jump to 2 NT over a 1♢ opening:

(a)   ♠ Q x x   ♡ J x x x x   ♢ J x   ♣ x x x

The partner of the 2 NT bidder should pass.

(b)   ♠ Q J 10 x x x x   ♡ x x x   ♢ Q x   ♣ x

Worth a jump to 4♠.

Suit Overcalls

After a one-level opening, and overcall may be made at the one level if the suit of the overcall ranks higher than the suit opened.

If the suit of the overcall ranks lower than the suit opened, the overcall must be at the two level.

An overcall is a bid after the righthand opponent has bid or after both opponents have bid.*

STRENGTH REQUIRED FOR OVERCALL IN A SUIT

An overcall may be made for any of several reasons: it may be made in hopes of reaching a game; it may be made in hopes of taking up sufficient room to prevent the other side from easily finding its best contract; it may be made to suggest to the overcaller's partner an opening lead against the opponents' final contract. With this variety of goals, the point range of the overcall is necessarily wide.

An overcall at the one level can be made on as few as 9 and as many as 18 points.

*A bid after *only* the lefthand opponents has bid is called a "balancing" bid rather than an overcall. (See page 270.)

For safety's sake, an overcall at the two level should have at least the high card values needed for a minimum opening bid; its range is thus 13-18 points.

And an overcall after a 1 NT opening bid should be the soundest of all, for it is easiest for the partner of the NT opener to determine which side has the majority of strength and whether or not to double for penalties.

A would-be overcaller should also take into account the vulnerability. He can afford to make a lighter overcall if he is not vulnerable, but usually cannot if he is vulnerable.

If the opponents are not vulnerable, it becomes more attractive for them to double and try to collect a penalty than if they are vulnerable. Thus, greater care should be taken if the opponents are not vulnerable.

Examples:

(a) ♠ x x   ♡ K Q J x x   ♢ K x x   ♣ x x x

Worth a 1♡ overcall over a 1♣ or a 1◊ opening, if for no other reason than to direct partner toward the lead of a heart. The texture of the suit is sufficiently solid that a 1♡ overcall is justifiable regardless of the vulnerability. The hand is not, however, strong enough to warrant an overcall at the two level at any vulnerability if the opening bid has been 1♠. Over a 1♠ opening, therefore, pass.

(b) ♠ A K Q x x x   ♡ A x x   ♢ Q x x   ♣ x

This is the maximum end of the range of a non-jump overcall. Here, the hope is that the overcaller's partner will be able to invite game or accept a game invitation should overcaller get the opportunity to issue one.

(c)   ♠ x   ♡ A Q J x x   ◊ A K x x x   ♣ x x

Worth a 1♡ overcall over a 1♣ opening or a 2♡ overcall over a 1♠ opening. Overcaller hopes to be able to show his diamond suit later.

An overcall after both opponents have bid should not be made unless the hand has at least the strength of an opening bid, for it is far easier for the opponents to inflict a penalty on the overcaller when each of them has already commenced to describe his hand.

LENGTH REQUIRED
FOR SUIT OF OVERCALL

The suit of the overcall should, except in rare cases, be at least five cards long.

The fact that a player has a second suit should encourage him to make an overcall. Two-suited hands are safer to intervene with than one-suited hands, since normally partner will have support for one of the two suits.

SUIT TEXTURE REQUIRED
FOR SUIT OVERCALL

An overcall should not be made in a suit unless the suit itself is reasonably strong. A suit of five cards headed by the King and Jack or the Q J 10 is the minimum on which an overcall should be made. With less than K J x x x or Q J 10 x x, there is little obvious lead directional value, and no particular reason to think that this suit will be the best denomination in which to play the hand.

If the overcall is to be made at the two level, the suit shoud be of even better length or quality, such as K Q 10 x x or K J x x x x.

CHOOSING BETWEEN AN OVERCALL AND A TAKEOUT DOUBLE

With length in all three unbid suits, a player should compare the value of overcalling with the benefit to be gained from making a takeout double.

The doubt should usually be resolved in favor of the overcall, if it can be made at the one level and the suit is sound. If the suit is weak, a takeout double may be more appropriate.

Examples:

(a)　♠ A K x x　♡ Q x x x x　◊ x　♣ A x x

The heart suit is not strong enough to warrant an overcall of 1♡ over 1◊, especially with length and strength in clubs and spades as well. Therefore, a takeout double should be preferred.

(b)　♠ K x x x　♡ A K J x x　◊ x　♣ Q x x

Although this hand has the same distribution and same point count as hand (a), it should be overcalled 1♡ because of the texture of the heart suit.

RESPONSES TO NON-JUMP OVERCALLS

In responding to an overcall, the overcaller's partner should bear in mind that his partner has promised a reasonably sound suit. There is rarely, therefore, any reason for overcaller's partner to try to find a better denomination if he has a weak hand. Any bid by the overcaller's partner, therefore, should be constructive and show interest in trying for game.

Once an opponent's bid has revealed the location of most of the missing high cards, game becomes a worthwhile proposition with as few as 25 points.

RAISING THE OVERCALLER'S SUIT

A raise of the suit of the overcall may be made with three small cards in support, or even with as little as Q x if necessary. Since the overcaller has shown a good five-card suit, such holdings constitute adequate support.

In determining how high to raise, attention must be paid to the vulnerability. Since overcaller may not have a full opening bid if he is non-vulnerable, greater strength is needed in raising non-vulnerable overcalls.

A raise to the two level is somewhat encouraging. It normally promises about 8-10 points in support of overcaller's suit if the partnership is vulnerable, or 10-12 if non-vulnerable.

A raise to the three level is very encouraging, but is not forcing. It promises about 11-12 points vulnerable, or 13-15 points non-vulnerable.

A raise to the four level is strong, promising 13-15 points vulnerable, or 15-17 points non-vulnerable.

Examples—Facing an overcall of 1♠ over 1◇ :

(a)   ♠ Q x   ♡ x x x x   ◇ x x   ♣ A K x x x

Worth a raise to 2♠ regardless of the vulnerability. There is no point in introducing the club suit, for overcaller's suit rates to be as strong.

(b)   ♠ K x x x   ♡ A Q x x   ◊ x   ♣ x x x x

Worth a raise to 3♠ if vulnerable, but only to 2♠ non-vulnerable.

RESPONDING IN A NEW SUIT

The bid of a new suit by the overcaller's partner is not forcing. Nevertheless, it normally promises a hand worth at least 9 points, usually with a suit that is itself good enough for an overcall. The bid of a new suit suggests that the overcaller's partner has at most a weak doubleton in the overcaller's suit.

If the new suit is bid at the one level, it may be only five cards long. If it must be bid at the two level, it promises at least six cards.

A jump by the overcaller's partner in a new suit is forcing for one round. It is the recommended course of action when the hand contains inadequate support for overcaller's suit, but enough strength to make game worth investigation.

Examples—Facing a 1♡ overcall over a 1♣ opening:

(a)   ♠ Q x x x x   ♡ x   ◊ A x x   ♣ x x x x

Should be passed because it is too weak to suggest exploration of game possibilities, and because there is no reason to believe that spades will be a better trump suit than hearts.

(b)   ♠ A Q J x x   ♡ x x   ◊ K x x   ♣ x x x

The overcaller's partner should bid 1♠, hoping that overcaller can raise. The one spade bid is not forcing.

(c)   ♠ A K x x x x   ♡ x   ◊ A K x x   ♣ x x

*The one spade bid should not be risked with a hand as
strong as this one. The overcaller's partner should jump to
2♠, forcing overcaller to bid again.*

RESPONDING WITH A CUE-BID

A bid in the opponent's suit by the partner of the overcaller shows a
hand that may be strong enough for game, but that does not clearly
suggest in what denomination to play.

The cue-bid is forcing for one round, but is not forcing to game.
If the partner of the overcaller bids a new suit after cue-bidding, his
second bid is forcing to game.

Example—Facing a 1♡ overcall over a 1♢ opening:

(a)   ♠ A K J x x   ♡ x   ♢ Q x x   ♣ A K x x

*A 2♢ cue-bid should be made. If the overcaller rebids 2♡,
this hand should bid 2♠.*

RESPONDING IN NOTRUMP

If the overcaller's partner has insufficient support for overcaller's
suit and has no really good suit of his own to bid, but yet has 9 or
more points, and thus wants to make a constructive bid, he should
respond in NT if he has a stopper in the suit opened. These responses, like raises, must take into account the fact that non-vulnerable
the overcaller may have less than an opening bid.

**A 1 NT response promises 9-10 points if vulnerable, or 9-12
points non-vulnerable.**

A 2 NT response vaies not only according to the vulnerability, but also according to the level at which the overcall was made.

If the overcall was made at the one level, a 2 NT response promises 11-12 points vulnerable or 13-14 points non-vulnerable.

If the overcall was made at the two level, the 2 NT response promises 10-11 points vulnerable or 12-13 points non-vulnerable.

A 3 NT response promises 13-16 points vulnerable, or 15-16 non-vulnerable.

Examples—Facing a 1♠ overcall over a 1♢ opening:

(a)   ♠ xx   ♡ xxxx   ♢ AKxx   ♣ xxx

Should be passed, because it is not strong enough to warrant any action.

(b)   ♠ x   ♡ K 10 xx   ♢ KQxx   ♣ Kxxx

Worth a 1 NT response non-vulnerable, or a jump to 2 NT vulnerable.

(c)   ♠ xx   ♡ AKxx   ♢ Jxx   ♣ AKxx

Not suitable for a NT bid because it lacks a diamond stopper. Nor can overcaller's suit be raised, nor a new suit be bid. The only course of action is to cue-bid opener's suit.

SECOND BID BY OVERCALLER

After a raise or a NT response, overcaller's task is a relatively simple one, for these bids show fairly precise point ranges. Overcaller simply adds his own points to those promised by his partner.

AFTER A NOTRUMP RESPONSE

If the response was in NT, overcaller can sign off by passing or by rebidding his suit if it is six cards long.

The bid of a new suit is mildly forward-going, but is not forcing. If overcaller has a two-suited hand worth 15 or more points, he should jump in his second suit. This bid is forcing for one round, but is not forcing to game.

AFTER A RAISE OF OVERCALLER'S SUIT

If his partner has raised his overcall, overcaller can sign off by passing. Any other action by overcaller, such as the bid of a new suit, is a mild continuation of the exploration of game possibilities.

AFTER A RESPONSE IN A NEW SUIT

After overcaller's partner has made a non-jump response in a new suit, overcaller should raise his partner's suit if he has three-card support, even if he has minimum strength, since the new suit bid has a wide point range.

If overcaller has a minimum and less than three-card support, he should pass.

With substantially better than a minimum, overcaller should bid again even without a fit for his partner's suit. His choices include bidding NT with stoppers in opener's suit and the unbid suit, bidding a new suit with a two-suited hand, and rebidding his own suit if it contains six or more cards.

After overcaller's partner has jumped in a new suit, overcaller must bid once more. If he has J x or better in his partner's suit, he should raise. Otherwise, he should bid NT if he has opener's suit stopped, or bid a new suit if he has a two-suited hand, or rebid his suit if it is six or more cards long.

AFTER A CUE-BID

After a cue-bid by his partner, overcaller should bid a second suit if he has one, or bid NT if he has a stopper in opener's suit, or rebid his own suit. If he has a good six-card suit, overcaller should jump rebid his suit; if he rebids his suit without a jump and his partner raises, he may pass.

Example:

North	East	South	West
1♣	1♡	Pass	2♣
Pass	2♠	Pass	3♡

In this auction, West's 3♡ bid is not forcing.

REQUIREMENTS FOR A SUIT OVERCALL AFTER THE OPPONENTS HAVE REACHED THE TWO LEVEL OR HIGHER

To overcall over an opening bid made at the two level or higher, or after an opening bid and a response at the two level or higher, a player should have a very sound hand and a sound suit.

When the opponents have already reached the two or three level, an overcall should not be made without at least 16 points.

The player making such an overcall promises a suit that is either longer or stronger than the minimum needed for a one-level overcall. The K J x x x suit with which he might overcall at the one level does not provide adequate safety if he must bid at the three level; such a ragged suit is very much easier for the opponents to double for penalties at the three level than at the one level.

The minimum suit holding for an overcall above the one level should be K Q 10 x x. Lacking such a suit, a takeout double should be considered.

JUMP OVERCALLS IN SUITS

A single jump overcall in a suit shows a hand with a strong suit and about 15-17 points. The suit should be solid or at least semi-solid. The hand may contain a second suit that can be shown later in the bidding.

Examples:

(a) ♠ A x   ♡ x x   ◇ K x   ♣ A K J x x x x

Qualifies for a jump to 3♣ over any opening bid.

(b) ♠ A Q J x x x   ♡ K Q x   ◇ x   ♣ A x x

A jump to 2♠ would be appropriate.

RESPONSES TO JUMP OVERCALLS

If the partner of the jump overcaller has a hand worth 8-9 points, he should bid. If the overcall was at the three level, he should bid a game. After a jump to the two level, he should make a game try with 8-9 points, and bid a game or force to game with 10 or more points.

Since the overcall has shown a solid or semi-solid suit, there is no point in introducing a new suit. Hence, the partner of the overcaller should limit himself to raising the overcaller's suit or bidding NT.

The partner of the overcaller should generally raise the overcaller's suit if he has two-card or longer support and it is a major suit.

With a stopper in opener's suit, overcaller's partner should bid NT if he has a singleton in the suit of the overcall or if the suit is a minor.

Examples:

(a)   ♠ x x   ♡ A x x   ◊ A x x   ♣ x x x x x

Facing a jump to 2♠ over a 1◊ opening, the overcaller's partner should jump to 4♠; his two Aces and two-card support should suffice to produce a game.

(b)   ♠ x x   ♡ J x x x   ◊ K J x   ♣ Q J x x

Facing a jump to 2♠ over a 1◊ opening, the partner of overcaller should content himself with a bid of 2 NT, since his values are soft. The 2 NT response allows the overcaller to pass with a minimum and no singleton, or to rebid three of his suit with a minimum and a singleton, or to bid game with a maximum, either in NT or in his own suit.

(c)   ♠ Q x x   ♡ K J x   ◊ Q x x x   ♣ x x x

Facing a 3♣ jump overcall over a 1♡ opening, the partner of the overcaller should bid 3 NT.

HIGHER JUMP OVERCALLS

A double jump or higher overcall (e.g., 3♠ over 1♦, 4♠ over 1♣, 4♣ over 1♡) is a pre-emptive bid that promises a long suit and fewer than 10 high card points.

The Rule of Two and Three should be followed: if vulnerable, the jump overcaller should have playing strength that is within two tricks of his contract; if non-vulnerable, he should be within three tricks of his contract.

Takeout Doubles

A takeout double does not seek to penalize the opponents, but instead asks the doubler's partner to bid an unbid suit. The takeout double may be made with a wide variety of hands, and may be made after either or both of the opponents have bid.

The discussion in this section applies only if righthand opponent or both opponents have bid.

DISTINGUISHING A ONE-LEVEL TAKEOUT DOUBLE FROM A PENALTY DOUBLE

At the one level it is relatively easy to know when a double is takeout or penalty.

A double of any suit bid is takeout if the partner of the doubler has not bid, so long as there are at least two unbid suits.

A double of 1 NT response to an opening bid is also for takeout if the doubler's partner has not bid.

A double of any other NT bid is a penalty double, regardless of whether or not the doubler's partner has bid.

A double of any bid in a suit is a penalty double if the doubler's partner has bid.

Examples:

(a)
North	East	South	West
1♣	Pass	1♠	Pass
1 NT	Double		

The double is a penalty double. East must have a very strong club holding.

(b)
North	East	South	West
1◇	Pass	1♡	Double

The double is takeout since East has not bid.

(c)
North	East	South	West
1♣	1♡	1♠	Double

The double is for penalties since East has already bid.

STRENGTH AND DISTRIBUTION REQUIRED FOR TAKEOUT DOUBLES OF A SUIT BID OF ONE

To make a takeout double of a one-level opening, a player should have at least three cards in every unbid suit. In addition, since the doubler's partner may have to respond with no points at all, the doubler should have a fair hand—at least 13 points counting high cards and distribution.

Usually the doubler promises shortness in opener's suit, and the more cards he has in opener's suit, the more high card strength he needs to compensate.

In addition, the more likely it is that the doubler's partner will have to respond at the two level rather than the one level (because of the rank of the suit opened), the more strength the doubler should have. Thus, the double of a 1♣ opening does not require as great strength as the double of 1♠.

Examples:

(a)   ♠ K x x x   ♡ A x x x   ◇ x   ♣ A x x x

A takeout double of 1◇ is appropriate.

(b)   ♠ x x   ♡ K x x x   ◇ A x x x   ♣ A x x

If the opening bid is 1♠, the hand is not quite strong enough for a takeout double, since the doubler's partner would be forced to bid at the two level.

(c)   ♠ x x x   ♡ K Q x   ◇ A x x x   ♣ A Q x

Appropriate for a takeout double of 1♠, despite the three-card length in opener's suit, since the hand contains compensating high card strength.

A takeout double may also be made with a hand that is too strong for a simple overcall in a suit or in NT. In these cases, the doubler may not have support for every unbid suit, but he intends to clarify his hand on his next turn.

Examples:

(d)   ♠ A K Q x x x   ♡ A x x   ◇ A x x   ♣ x

Too strong for a simple overcall of 1♠ over 1♣. The appropriate action is a takeout double and a bid in spades on the next round.

(e)   ♠ Q x   ♡ A Q x x   ◇ A K x   ♣ K Q x x

Too strong for a 1 NT overcall over a 1 ◇ opening. The appropriate action is a takeout double and a non-jump bid in NT on the next round, showing 20-21 high card points.

RESPONSES TO TAKEOUT DOUBLES

Doubler's partner is required to bid in response to the double unless he believes he can set the opening bid by more than the value of whatever contract his side can make.

If he has such a belief, he may pass; otherwise, he must bid. His options include bids in a new suit, bids in NT, and cue-bids of opener's suit.

The cue-bid is the only bid that is forcing in response to a takeout double.

RESPONDING TO TAKEOUT DOUBLE
WITH A NON-JUMP BID IN A NEW SUIT

A non-jump response in an unbid suit, if the double has been followed by an opponent's pass, does not promise any strength whatever. It may be made with zero points, because the double has forced him to bid.

The upper limit of the non-jump suit response is 8 points.

Examples—Facing a takeout double of 1 ◇ :

(a)   ♠ x x x   ♡ x x x x   ◇ x x x   ♣ x x x

Doubler's partner should bid 1 ♡ .

(b)   ♠ Q x x   ♡ A J x x   ◊ x x x   ♣ x x x

Doubler's partner should bid 1♡ .

If the double has been followed by a bid by righthand opponent, a bid by doubler's partner promises 7-8 points, although it may be made with as few as 6 points at the one level with a five-card suit.

Example:

(c)   ♠ x x   ♡ K Q x x x   ◊ x x x   ♣ x x x

Worth a response of 1♡ to a takeout double of 1♣ if righthand opponent has passed or if he has bid 1◊. However, if righthand opponent has bid 1♠, this hand is a bit short for a free bid at the two level and should be passed.

The doubler's partner should usually respond in his longest unbid suit. Sometimes this will be a five-card or longer suit; most often it will be a four-card suit; on occasion, it will be a three-card suit.

his longest unbid suit occurs when he has a weak hand and a four-card major suit that he can bid at the one level, and a five-card minor suit he would have to go to the two level to bid. In this event, doubler's partner should bid his four-card major suit in preference to raising the level.

Examples:

(d)   ♠ x x x x   ♡ x x   ◊ x x x x x   ♣ x x

Facing a takeout double of 1◊ , doubler's partner should bid 1♠ , his longest unbid suit.

(e)   ♠ x x   ♡ x x x x   ◇ x x   ♣ Q x x x x

Facing a takeout double of 1◇, doubler's partner should respond 1♡, his four-card suit, rather than 2♣, his five-card suit. Because his hand is very weak, he should avoid going to the two level, since he has a four-card major he can bid more cheaply.

(f)   ♠ Q x x x   ♡ x x   ◇ J x x x x   ♣ x x

After a takeout double of 1♣, doubler's partner should respond 1◇, his longest suit, since he can do so at the one level.

When the partner of the doubler has two suits of equal length, his choice of which to bid first depends on the rank of his suits and the strength of his hand.

If doubler's partner has equal length in a major and a minor, he should generally bid the major suit.

If his two equally long suits are both majors or both minors, he should determine which suit to bid based on what the precise length is and what his strength is.

If he is choosing between two three-card suits, he should bid the cheaper.

If he is choosing between two five-card suits, he should bid the higher ranking, intending to bid the lower on the next round.

If he has two four-card suits, he should bid the cheaper if his hand is weak (0-6 points), and should bid the higher with 7 or 8 points, planning to bid the lower at his next turn.

Examples:

(g)   ♠ A x x   ♡ J x x   ◊ x x x x   ♣ Q x x

Facing a takeout double of 1◊, the doubler's partner must choose among three-card suits. He should respond 1♡, his cheapest suit.

(h)   ♠ K x x x   ♡ J x x x   ◊ x x x   ♣ x x

Facing a takeout double of 1◊, doubler's partner should bid 1♡, since his hand is weak.

(i)   ♠ K x x x   ♡ A x x x   ◊ x x x   ♣ x x

Facing a takeout double of 1◊, doubler's partner is strong enough for two bids and thus should respond 1♠, intending to bid hearts at his next turn.

(j)   ♠ Q x   ♡ x x x   ◊ A x x x   ♣ K x x x

Opposite a takeout double of 1♡, doubler's partner should respond 2◊, planning to bid clubs at his next turn.

NON-JUMP SUIT BIDS OVER A REDOUBLE

If the double has been followed by a redouble, doubler's partner is no longer required to bid. A pass over the redouble indicates a willingness to have the doubler bid any of the unbid suits, especially the higher ranking.

However, if doubler's partner has a preference for one of the unbid suits, he should bid that suit.

The bid of a new suit over a redouble does not promise any strength.

RESPONDING TO TAKEOUT DOUBLE
WITH A JUMP IN A NEW SUIT

A single jump in a new suit by doubler's partner promises 9-11 points and at least a good four-card suit. While the jump response is encouraging, it is not forcing.

Example:

(a)   ♠ A x x x x   ♡ x   ◊ K x x x   ♣ J x x

Worth a jump to 2♠ over a takeout double.

A double jump or higher jump in a new suit by doubler's partner shows a hand that is weakish in high cards but long of suit—a maximum of 9 high card points, with at least a six-card suit. These jumps suggest that the contract bid can be made opposite a minimum takeout double.

Examples:

(b)   ♠ Q J x x x x   ♡ x x   ◊ A x x   ♣ x x

Opposite a takeout double of 1♣, 1◊, or 1♡, this hand is worth a jump to 3♠.

(c)   ♠ K x x x x x x   ♡ x   ◊ K x   ♣ x x x

Doubler's partner should jump to 4♠ over a takeout double.

RESPONDING TO TAKEOUT DOUBLE IN NOTRUMP

A NT response to a takeout double promises a stopper in opener's suit and a relatively balanced hand. The NT response is never made for the sole purpose of showing the stopper, however; it promises a hand that has some strength as well.

A response of 1 NT by doubler's partner promises 8-10 points.

A response of 2 NT promises 11-12 points.

A response of 3 NT promises 13-16 points.

If doubler's partner has both a stopper in opener's suit and a five-card suit of his own, he should bid his suit if his hand either is only semi-balanced or has a weak stopper.

Examples—Opposite a takeout double of 1 ◊ :

(a)   ♠ x x x   ♡ x x x   ◊ K Q x x x   ♣ x x

Doubler's partner should bid 1♡, since he lacks the high card strength to bid 1 NT.

(b)   ♠ A x x x x   ♡ K x   ◊ Q x x x   ♣ x x

Doubler's partner should bid 2♠ rather than 1 NT because his hand is only semi-balanced and because he has only one diamond stopper at best.

(c)   ♠ x x   ♡ K J x x   ◊ Q x x   ♣ Q x x x

Bid 1♡ because of the weakness of the diamond holding.

(d)   ♠ x x   ♡ K x x   ◊ A J x x   ♣ K x x x

Jump to 2 NT.

RESPONDING TO TAKEOUT DOUBLE WITH A CUE-BID

A cue-bid by the doubler's partner promises that the partnership has game, but suggests that he does not know in what denomination to play. The cue-bid promises at least 12 points, but does not promise anything about the holding in opener's suit. The cue-bid is the only forcing response to a takeout double.

Examples:

(a) ♠ A x x x   ♡ K Q x x   ◇ K x   ♣ x x x

(b) ♠ A x   ♡ Q J x x   ◇ A K x   ♣ x x x x

Opposite a takeout double of 1♣, doubler's partner might have either hand (a) or (b) for a cue-bid of 2♣.

RESPONDING TO A TAKEOUT DOUBLE
WITH A PENALTY PASS

If doubler's partner believes that the partnership can earn more by defending against the opening bid than by seeking a contract of its own, he may pass the takeout double.

He must be aware of two factors, however, that argue against a penalty pass. First, the doubler is likely to have only a singleton in opener's suit. Second, doubler's partner is sitting in front of opener, so that opener may be able to finesse his trumps. Indeed, if he passes for penalties, doubler will lead a trump if he has one.

In order to pass the takeout double, therefore, doubler's partner should have long trumps and they should be reasonably solid. For example, K J 6 5 3 is not a solid enough trump holding, while Q J 10 9 x is. In addition, doubler's partner should have some high card strength outside the trump suit.

Examples—Facing a takeout double of 1♠:

(a)   ♠ K J 9 7 x   ♡ x   ♢ K Q x x   ♣ x x x

Doubler's partner should bid 2♢. His trumps are not quite strong enough for a penalty pass.

(b)   ♠ Q J 10 x x x   ♡ x x   ♢ x x   ♣ x x x

Doubler's partner should bid 2♣. He lacks the over-all strength needed to make a penalty pass.

(c)   ♠ K J 10 9 x   ♡ x x   ♢ A x x   ♣ x x x

Doubler's partner should pass.

SECOND BID BY TAKEOUT DOUBLER

When doubler's partner has bid and doubler's turn comes again, doubler must keep in mind that if his partner has jumped or made a free bid, or responded in NT, he has shown strength within a well-defined range. However, if he has made a non-free bid (i.e., he has bid over the opponent's pass) in a new suit, he may have no points at all.

REBID BY DOUBLER AFTER A NON-JUMP NEW SUIT RESPONSE BY HIS PARTNER

After a non-free bid, new suit response to the takeout double, showing 0-8 points, doubler needs a good deal more than a minimum hand to proceed any further.

A raise by doubler promises 17-18 points. A jump raise promises 19-20 points.

A bid in a new suit by doubler promises 18 points and a long good suit. Such a bid casts some doubt on doubler's support for the other suits.

A bid in NT by doubler shows a stopper in opener's suit and promises at least 20 high card points—more than the strength for an immediate 1 NT overcall.

A cue-bid by doubler of opener's suit promises 21 or more points in support of the suit bid by doubler's partner. It does not promise control of opener's suit.

Examples—If the bidding has started:

North	East	South	West
1♡	Double	Pass	1♠
Pass			

(a)   ♠ A x x x   ♡ x   ◇ K Q x x   ♣ A x x x

East should pass because he lacks sufficient strength to assure safety at the two level if West has a worthless hand.

(b)   ♠ K Q x x   ♡ x   ◇ A Q x x   ♣ A x x x

East should raise to 2♠.

(c)   ♠ A J x x   ♡ x   ◇ K Q x x   ♣ A K x x

East should raise to 3♠.

(d)   ♠ A K x x   ♡ x x   ◇ A Q x   ♣ A K x x

East should cue-bid 2♡, showing 21 points, planning to raise spades at his next turn.

REBID BY DOUBLER AFTER
A JUMP RESPONSE IN A NEW SUIT BY HIS PARTNER

After the partner of the doubler has jumped in a new suit, showing 9-11 points, the doubler need not bid again if he has a bare minimum for his takeout double.

If he has 14 or 15 points, he should try for game by raising his partner's suit or by bidding NT if he has stoppers in the opener's suit.

If he has 16 or more points, doubler should assure that game is reached, either by jumping to game in his partner's suit with four-card support, or by bidding 3 NT with solid stoppers in opener's suit, or by cue-bidding opener's suit if he has neither of the above holdings.

Examples—If the auction has begun:

North	East	South	West
1 ◊	Double	Pass	2 ♠
Pass			

(a)   ♠ K J x x   ♡ Q x x x   ◊ x   ♣ A Q x x

East should raise to 3 ♠.

(b)   ♠ Q x x   ♡ K x x x   ◊ A Q   ♣ K J x x

East should bid 2 NT.

(c)   ♠ A x x x x   ♡ K Q x   ◊ x   ♣ A J x x

East should jump to game in spades.

(d)   ♠ Q x x   ♡ A K J x   ◊ x x   ♣ A Q x x

East should cue-bid 3 ◊. His partner should bid 3 NT if he has diamond stopper.

REBID BY DOUBLER AFTER
A NOTRUMP RESPONSE BY HIS PARTNER

After doubler's partner has responded in NT, doubler can simply add his own points to those promised by the response in determining whether or not to bid further. If the partnership has 25 high card points, game has good prospects since the opening bid has revealed the location of most of the missing cards.

Examples:

(a)   ♠ A Q x x   ♡ K x x x   ◇ x   ♣ A Q x x

Having made a takeout double of a 1◇ opening, and his partner having responded 1 NT, showing 8-10 points, the doubler should raise to 2 NT, inviting his partner to bid game with 10 points. If his partner had responded 2 NT to the takeout double, showing 11-12 points, doubler would raise to 3 NT.

(b)   ♠ K Q x   ♡ A Q x x   ◇ J x   ♣ K Q x x

After a takeout double of a 1◇ opening, and partner having responded 1 NT, the doubler should raise to 3 NT.

REBID BY DOUBLER AFTER
A CUE-BID RESPONSE BY HIS PARTNER

After doubler's partner has cue-bid, suggesting that game can be made, but seeking further information as to the appropriate denomination, doubler should bid a five-card suit if he has one, or should bid NT if he has no five-card suit but has a stopper in opener's suit. If he cannot take either of the above actions, the doubler may make a further cue-bid. After such a cue-bid, the doubler's partner should bid a four-card suit if he has one.

Examples—If the auction has begun:

North	East	South	West
1♣	Double	Pass	2♣
Pass			

(a)   ♠ A J x x   ♡ K x x x x   ◇ K x x   ♣ x

East should bid 2♡.

(b)   ♠ A J x x   ♡ K x x x   ◇ x x   ♣ K Q x

East should bid 2 NT.

(c)   ♠ A J x x   ♡ K x x x   ◇ K J x   ♣ x x

East should bid 3♣.

TAKEOUT DOUBLE OF BIDS ABOVE THE ONE LEVEL

Through the 4♡ level, the rules for distinguishing takeout doubles from penalty doubles above the one level are virtually the same as those applicable at the one level.

Any double of any suit bid below the game level, if the doubler's partner has not bid, is for takeout so long as there are at least two unbid suits.

A double of a 4♡ opening bid or response is for takeout if the doubler's partner has not bid.

A double of any bid in a suit is a penalty double if the doubler's partner has bid.

A double of any NT bid above the one level is for penalties.

A double of an opening bid or response of 4♠ or anything higher is for penalties, even if the doubler's partner has not bid.

Because of the strictures on overcalls above the one level, the takeout double at such a level may be made on a wider variety of hands than is normally the case at the one level. The principal requirements are that the doubler have a hand worth at least 16 points, and that he have at least three-card support for any unbid major suit.

Examples:

(a)   ♠ AKxxx   ♡ x   ♢ AQxx   ♣ Kxx

A 3♠ overcall is appropriate if the bidding has been opened with 3♣ by righthand opponent, or if a 1♣ opening by lefthand opponent has been raised to 3♣. If the opening were 3♡, however, or if a 1♡ opening had been raised to 3♡, a takeout double would be more appropriate. Even though the spade suit is sufficiently strong for an overcall, it is better to offer partner a choice of denominations with high cards and length in all of the unbid suits.

(b)   ♠ Qxxxx   ♡ AQx   ♢ AKJ   ♣ xx

This hand is strong enough for action over a 3♣ opening or raise, but the spade suit is too weak for an overcall. A takeout double should be made.

(c)   ♠ A x x   ♡ A x x   ◇ A K x   ♣ A x x x

Has enough high card points for a 3 NT overcall over any three-level opening or response. However, the hand has few playing tricks and a takeout double should be preferred.

Penalty Doubles

A penalty double is a call of "double" that means the doubler be-lieves the opponents cannot make the contract they have just bid. The double seeks to increase the penalty for their predicted failure.

GENERAL REQUIREMENTS FOR PENALTY DOUBLES

In general, the appropriateness of a penalty double depends not on point count, but on a variety of other factors such as:

- —the height of the contract;
- —the number of defensive tricks held by doubler;
- —the number of defensive tricks doubler should expect from his partner;
- —the doubler's length in trumps;
- —the doubler's length in his partner's suit;
- —the doubler's length in his own suit;
- —the doubler's length in declarer's side suit;
- —the doubler's length in dummy's side suit.

In counting defensive tricks, a player should take into account his position relative to the supposed location of the opponent's high cards. For example, the King of a suit bid on the player's right is more likely to be a winner than if it is in a suit bid on his left.

In general, a player should have four or more trumps to make a penalty double, although if the final contract is at the four level or higher, fewer trumps may suffice if enough high cards are held by the defense.

A player should beware of doubling when he has length in his partner's suit.

In deciding whether or not to make a penalty double of a part-score contract a player must also consider whether or not game will be scored if the contract doubled is made. Thus, if the contract is a part-score of 2♡ or higher, the doubler should be able to envision at least a two-trick defeat, both as a margin of safety and as a suitable reward for the hazard involved. The risk that a doubled 4♣ contract, for example, will be made at a cost of several hundred points, must be offset by the strong probability that 4♣ will be defeated and that its defeat will earn several hundred points.

NATURE OF DOUBLE: PENALTY vs. TAKEOUT

NATURE OF DOUBLES OF OPENING BIDS

There are a few opening bids the doubles of which are for penalties rather than takeout. These are double of NT openings and doubles of bids of 4♣ and higher.

The doubles of any suit opening from 1♣ through 4♡ *are takeout doubles.*

NATURE OF DOUBLES OF NOTRUMP BIDS

With one exception, the double of any NT bid is a penalty double.

The one exception is for a double of a 1 NT response to an opening bid if the partner of the doubler has not bid. Such a double is for takeout.

Examples:

(a)
North	East	South	West
1♡	Pass	1 NT	Double

West's double is for takeout. He promises length in all suits except hearts.

(b)
North	East	South	West
1◇	Double	1 NT	Double

West's double is for penalties since his partner has already bid.

(c)
North	East	South	West
1♣	Pass	1♡	Pass
1 NT	Double		

East's double is for penalties.

NATURE OF DOUBLES OF BIDS
OTHER THAN OPENING BIDS AND NOTRUMP BIDS

Any double after the partner of the doubler has bid or doubled is a penalty double.

Any double after three or four suits have been bid is a penalty double.

Any double of a suit over which the doubler has previously had an opportunity to make a takeout double is a penalty double.

Any double of a bid of 4♠ and above is a penalty double.

Any double of an artificial bid or a cue-bid is a penalty double.

Examples:

(a) | North | East | South | West |
|---|---|---|---|
| 1 NT | Pass | 2♣ | Double |

West's double of South's Stayman bid is for penalties.

(b) | North | East | South | West |
|---|---|---|---|
| 1♡ | Pass | 4♡ | Double |

West's double of 4♡ is primarily for takeout rather than penalties. If the auction had been 1♠-Pass-4♠, the double would have been for penalties.

(c) | North | East | South | West |
|---|---|---|---|
| 1♣ | Pass | 1◇ | Pass |
| 2♣ | Double | | |

East's double of 2♣ is for penalties.

(d) | North | East | South | West |
|---|---|---|---|
| 1♡ | Pass | 1♠ | Pass |
| 2♣ | Double | | |

East's double of 2♣ is for penalties since there is only one unbid suit.

REQUIREMENTS FOR
PENALTY DOUBLES
IN SPECIFIC TYPES OF AUCTIONS

All penalty doubles should meet, as closely as possible, the general requirements for penalty doubles. Some types of auctions occure frequently enough that penalty doubles of certain bids have come to be quite well defined. Others require more on-the-spot judgment.

REQUIREMENTS FOR
PENALTY DOUBLES OF NOTRUMP OPENINGS

A double of a 1 NT opening promises 16-18 high card points with good prospects for establishing seven tricks, or a good hand with a long suit that will produce the needed tricks.

Either of the following hands would be appropriate:

(a)   ♠ A K   ♡ Q J 10 x x   ◊ K Q x   ♣ K x x

(b)   ♠ A x x   ♡ x x   ◊ A K Q J 10 x x   ♣ x

With a balanced 16-18 point hand without a safe opening lead, however, or without a good suit to provide tricks, it is advisable to pass.

The following hand is not a good double of a 1 NT opening:

(c)   ♠ A x x   ♡ A Q x x   ◊ K J x   ♣ K J x

A double of a 2 NT or 3 NT opening has no precise relationship to the point count, but merely promises a source of tricks sufficient to defeat the contract.

The partner of the player who doubles an opening NT bid is expected to pass unless he has a virtually worthless hand and a long suit. He should rarely bid over the double.

REQUIREMENTS FOR
PENALTY DOUBLES OF VERY HIGH PRE-EMPTS

A double of an opening bid in a suit at the level of 4♠ or higher is based on Aces and trump tricks sufficient to defeat the contract.

In counting his potential tricks, the doubler must take into account the fact that the pre-empter will be short in the side suits. He must not rely on being able to take more than two tricks in any suit, and not more than one in any suit in which he himself holds five or more cards.

Examples—over an opening 4♠ pre-empt by righthand opponent:

(a)   ♠ K 10 9 x   ♡ A x x   ◇ A x x   ♣ A x x

Should double 4♠.

(b)   ♠ A x x   ♡ A K J x x x   ◇ x   ♣ K Q x

Should bid 5♡.

(c)   ♠ x   ♡ A Q J x x   ◇ K Q x x   ♣ A Q x

Should bid 4 NT for takeout.

REQUIREMENTS FOR
PENALTY DOUBLES OF NOTRUMP OVERCALLS

The double by responder of a 1 NT overcall promises at least 9 high card points.

The premise of the doubler is that his side has 22 or more points, leaving the overcaller with virtually all the rest and overcaller's partner with nothing.

Responder should be wary, however, of doubling with a freakish hand or one with which the NT overcaller is likely to be able to run a long suit.

REQUIREMENTS FOR
PENALTY DOUBLES OF SUIT OVERCALLS

In order to make a penalty double of an overcall in a suit, the doubler should have a hand worth at least a game invitation opposite the strength shown by his partner's bid. He should have at least four cards in the opponent's suit, with much of his strength concentrated in that suit; and he should have no more than three cards (and preferably fewer) in his partner's suit.

Examples:

(a) ♠ J x x   ♡ K Q 10 9   ◊ A 10 x x   ♣ x x

Opposite a 1♣ opening bid, responder has a good penalty double of a 1♡ overcall. If the opening bid were 1◊, however, a penalty double would be inadvisable because of responder's length in his partner's suit.

(b) *(North)* ♠ A Q 10 8   ♡ x x   ◊ A K x x x   ♣ K x

In the auction:

North	East	South	West
1◊	Pass	1♡	1♠

North should double 1♠ for penalties.

(c)   *(North)*   ♠ A x x x   ♡ x   ◊ K Q x x   ♣ A K x x

In the auction:

North	East	South	West
1 ◊	Pass	1 ♠	2 ♣

North should not double the 2♣ bid, despite the fact that the club suit is his strongest suit, for he has length in responder's suit. Instead, North should jump to 4♠, which South should have a reasonable chance of making, even holding a bare minimum.

REQUIREMENTS FOR
PENALTY DOUBLE OF OPPONENT'S CUE-BID

A double of a cue-bid is for penalties.

If the cue-bid was used in the standard way, showing a very strong hand, the double suggests that the doubler is short in his partner's suit and expects to penalize whatever suit the cue-bidder reveals.

If the cue-bid was of the modern variety, showing two suits and a weakish hand, the double suggests the ability to penalize at least one of the cue-bidder's two suits.

If the cue-bid was a control-showing cue-bid by a partnership that has shown game-going strength, the double is lead-directing; it suggests that the doubler's partner lead the suit of the cue-bid.

In addition, if the cue-bidder's side is vulnerable and the doubler's side is not, the double of the cue-bid suggests that a profitable sacrifice might be available in the suit of the cue-bid.

LEAD DIRECTING PENALTY DOUBLES

A lead directing penalty double is a double that asks the partner of the doubler to lead a particular suit against the final contract. A double of a final contract is normally lead directing only if it is made against a game or slam contract, although there are exceptions.

If the bid doubled is a cue-bid or an artificial bid, that is the suit that the doubler wants led. If the bid doubled is the final contract, there may be a question as to what lead is called for.

THE LIGHTNER DOUBLE OF A SLAM CONTRACT

A lead directing double of a voluntarily bid slam contract is called a Lightner double. The double requests an unusual lead and is normally made in the expectation of ruffing the suit led or of winning two top tricks in that suit.

The Lightner double precludes the lead of a trump. It also precludes the lead of any suit bid naturally by either of the defenders. In addition, it precludes the lead of a suit that has not been bid at all.

The Lightner double may call for dummy's first bid suit or for declarer's first bid suit. The opening leader should scrutinize his hand and deduce which unusual lead is called for.

Examples—If the auction has been:

North	East	South	West
1 ◊	Pass	1 ♡	Pass
2 ♠	Pass	4 ♠	Pass
6 ♠	Pass	Pass	Double

And East's hand is:

(a)   ♠ x x   ♡ x x x x x   ◊ x x x   ♣ x x x

(b)   ♠ x x   ♡ x x x   ◊ x x x x x   ♣ x x x

East should select a heart lead with hand (a) and a diamond lead with hand (b), in each case hoping that his great length means that West is void in the suit led.

West could have a hand such as:

(c)   ♠ A x   ♡ —   ◊ J x x x   ♣ Q x x x x x x

or (d)   ♠ A x   ♡ x x x x   ◊ —   ♣ J x x x x x x

DOUBLES OF SUIT GAME CONTRACTS

The double of a voluntarily bid game in a suit contract carries similar implications to the double of a slam contract. There may be hands on which the partner of the opening leader doubles the voluntarily bid game simply because he expects it to go down, even in the absence of a special lead. However, the doubler must have reason to believe that an "unusual" lead by the opening leader will not impair his ability to defeat the contract.

DOUBLES OF 3 NOTRUMP

The standard rules as to what suit is called for by the double of a 3 NT contract are as follows.

If the defending side (the doubler and/or the opening leader) has bid one and only one suit, the double calls for the lead of that suit.

If the doubler has bid a suit and the opening leader has bid another suit, the double calls for the lead of the suit bid by the opening leader.

If neither defender has bid, the double generally calls for the lead of the first suit bid by dummy. If dummy's suit has been strongly rebid, however, the double may not call for this lead or any other specific lead.

Example:

	North	East	South	West
(a)	1♣	Pass	1♡	Pass
	3♣	Pass	3 NT	Pass
	Pass	Double	Pass	Pass
	Pass			

The double by East is hardly likely to call for a club lead to defeat the contract. West should probably either lead a heart (declarer's suit) or lead from his own weakest suit.

If no suit has been bid by either the defenders or the declaring side, for example:

	North	East	South	West
(b)	1 NT	Pass	2 NT	Pass
	3 NT			

The double asks the opening leader to lead from his weakest short suit. The doubler implies that he has a running suit.

REDOUBLE OF PENALTY DOUBLE

After an opponent has made a penalty double of a bid that could systemically be the final contract in the absence of competition, a pass indicates a lack of desire or ability to try to improve the contract.

A redouble suggests great strength, and is an effort to increase the premium for the making of the doubled contract. It is *not*, without express agreement in advance, an S.O.S. asking partner to bid another suit.

A redouble implies that the doubling side will have no haven should they retreat from the redouble.

The bid of a new suit or NT after a penalty double is a sign of weakness. The only bid over a penalty double that shows strength is a cue-bid of a suit an opponent has bid strongly, or a "raise" of the denomination in which the penalty double is made.

Examples:

(a)	North	East	South	West
	1♠	2♣	2♠	Double
(b)	Redouble			
	1♠	2♣	Double	Redouble

In auctions (a) and (b), the redoubles show strength and confidence that the doubled contracts will be made.

(c)	North	East	South	West
	1♠	2♣	Double	2♦

West's 2♦ bid is not constructive. It promises a weak hand with a long diamond suit and probably a singleton or void in clubs.

(d)	North	East	South	West
	1 NT	Double	Redouble	

South's redouble indicates a willingness to play in 1NT; he promises at least 8-9 points and reasonably balanced distribution.

(e)	North	East	South	West
	1 NT	Double	2 NT	

South's 2 NT bid indicates a two-suited hand—one with which it was not safe to redouble since East might have a running suit of his own.

After an opponent has made a penalty double of an artificial bid at a low level, a redouble indicates a willingness to play in that contract. For example, in the Stayman auction:

(f)	North	East	South	West
	1 NT	Pass	2♣	Double
	Redouble			

Opener's redouble suggests that he has five clubs and is willing to play the contract of 2♣ redoubled.

After a penalty double of a cue-bid or an artificial bid at a high level of the auction, the redouble promises second-round control of the suit. It does not, however, suggest that the hand be played in that contract.

Examples:

(g)	North	East	South	West
	1♠	Pass	3♠	Pass
	4♣	Double	Redouble	

North has cue-bid in clubs showing first-round control. South's redouble promises second-round control of clubs.

(h)	North	East	South	West
	1♡	Pass	3♡	Pass
	4 NT	Pass	5◇	Double
	Pass	Pass	Redouble	

West has doubled South's Ace-showing response to Blackwood; North could bid or redouble himself if he were satis-
fied with the partnership's control of diamonds; his pass en-
ables South to redouble to show second-round control.

Cue-Bids in Opponent's Suits

A bid in a suit that an opponent has bid naturally is a cue-bid and is forcing.

STRENGTH REQUIRED FOR CUE-BIDS OF ONE LEVEL OPENINGS

The modern standard use of the cue-bid of an opening bid is to show a powerful hand, with or without first round control of opener's suit.

The cue-bid shows almost enough strength to force to game. It is made with a hand that is too strong for a simple overcall, and that is unsuitable for a takeout double. It may be made with a one-, two-, or three-suited hand.

Examples:

(a)   ♠ A K x x x x   ♡ —   ◇ A K x x x x   ♣ x

After a 1♡ opening by righthand opponent, a cue-bid of 2♡ should be made. The hand is too strong and distributional for either a simple overcall or a takeout double. The risk of an overcall is that it will be passed. The risk of a takeout double is that it, too, will be passed, with the opponents making 1♡ doubled while the defense is laydown for six-spades or six diamonds.

(b)   ♠ A x   ♡ A Q J x x x x   ◇ x   ♣ A J x

(c)   ♠ A K x x   ♡ A Q J x   ◇ —   ♣ A x x x x

With hands (b) and (c) a cue-bid of 2◇ over a 1◇ opening would be appropriate.

The meaning of the cue-bid is the same if the bidding has been opened by the cue-bidder's lefthand opponent and two passes have ensued. It is also the same if the bidding has been opened above the one level. It is nearly the same if there have been both an opening bid and a response; except there, the cue-bidder more often has a two-suiter rather than a one-suiter.

CUE-BID IN NOTRUMP

A bid of 2 NT over righthand opponent's 1 NT opening bid shows a two-suited hand with powerful playing strength. Any combination of suits is possible.

The bid normally shows a hand unsuited to a penalty double of 1 NT because the suits cannot be guaranteed to run and because of shortness in the other suits.

Example:

♠ A K x x x x x   ♡ x   ◊ K Q x x x   ♣ —

RESPONSES TO THE CUE-BID

The partner of the cue-bidder is expected to bid his longest suit, and await further identification of the cue-bidder's suit or suits.

After the cue-bidder's partner has bid a suit, a repeat cue-bid by the original cue-bidder asks his partner to choose between the two remaining suits.

Example:

North	East	South	West
1 ◊	2 ◊	Pass	3 ♣
Pass	3 ◊		

The 3 ◊ repeat cue-bid asks West to bid his better major suit. East could have a hand such as:

♠ A K x x x   ♡ K Q J x x   ◊ —   ♣ A Q x

If the cue-bidder simply bids a new suit over his partner's response to the cue-bid, it is not forcing.

Re-Opening the Bidding— "Balancing"

A re-opening or balancing call is a bid or double that is made after the opponents' bidding has stopped at a low level.

Examples—Typical auctions giving rise to balancing situations:

	North	East	South	West
(a)	1♡	Pass	Pass	
(b)	1♠	Pass	2♠	Pass
	Pass			
(c)	1◇	Pass	1 NT	Pass
	Pass			

In auction (a), West is in the position to balance (to re-open the bidding). In auctions (b) and (c), East is in the balancing position.

APPROPRIATENESS OF BALANCING

To warrant taking action in the balancing position, a player must be able to infer that his side possesses a reasonable amount of strength and a fit in some suit.

If the partner of the opening bidder has failed to keep the bidding open, it can be inferred that he has 0-5 points. Since opener's hand is in the 13-20 point range, the side that did not open the bidding should have a total of 15-27 points—or perhaps more if opener has counted on distributional values.

When there has been a minimum response to the opening bid (showing 6-9 points) and opener has failed to rebid (thereby showing 13-16 points), the side that did not open the bidding should have a minimum total of 15-21 points.

To determine whether or not a balancing action is likely to be advantageous, the player in balancing position looks principally to three factors.

The first is whether the opponents have demonstrably found a fit of their own. Their having found a fit increases the likelihood that the balancing side too has a fit.

In the following auction, the opponents have not clearly found a fit.

North	East	South	West
1♣	Pass	1♡	Pass
2♣	Pass	Pass	

Balancing would be somewhat dangerous.

The second factor is whether the player in balancing position has length in the opener's suit. If he does have length, it is likely that his partner does not. Yet if his partner is short in opener's suit and did not take action when it was his turn, he cannot have a very good suit or many high card points.

The third factor is whether the player in the balancing position holds a singleton in an unbid suit. If he does, it is likely that either his partner has length in that suit and his hand will not fit well with the balancer's suits, or that the opponents will be better off in balancer's short suit than in the suit they have bid.

WHAT BALANCING ACTION TO TAKE

Because the strength held by the opponents is limited, balancing bids and doubles of suit openings can appropriately be made with less strength than would be required for similar action over a bid by righthand opponent.

A non-jump balancing bid in a new suit promises 8-13 points. It may be made with a four-card suit.

A jump bid in a new suit in the balancing position promises 12-16 points with a six-card suit or a good five-card suit.

A 1 NT bid in the balancing position promises 11-14 high card points, a more or less balanced hand, and a stopper in opener's suit.

A takeout double in the balancing position is unlimited and has much the same meaning as an immediate double. It may be made on as few as 11 points if the balancer is short in opener's suit and has length in all of the unbid suits.

Because the strength of suit and NT balancing bids is limited, the takeout double may be made on any of a number of different hands. If he has other than an 11-14 point distributional takeout double, the balancer expects to clarify his holding at his next turn.

A cue-bid in the balancing position shows a hand with which the balancer is afraid his partner might make a penalty pass of a takeout double. Normally, it is a strong two-suited hand, although a three-suiter is also possible.

Examples:

(a)   ♠ x   ♡ A x x x   ◇ Q x x x   ♣ A x x x

After an opening bid of 1♠ by lefthand opponent has been

*followed by two passes, the player in balancing position
should make a balancing double. If, however, the bidding
has been opened with 1♡ rather than 1♠, this hand should
pass. The likelihood of a decent fit has been lessened by balancer's length in opener's suit and by balancer's partner's
failure to take action at his first turn.*

(b)   ♠ Q x x   ♡ Q J x x   ◇ A x x x   ♣ K x

*If the bidding has been opened with 1♡ by lefthand
opponent and there have been two passes, the proper bid is
1 NT, showing a stopper in opener's suit and 11-14 points.*

(c)   ♠ Q J x x   ♡ x x   ◇ A x x x x   ♣ Q x

*In the same auction as in example (b), the proper bid is 1♠,
showing 8-13 points. A 2◇ bid might well prevent the partnership from discovering a 4-4 spade fit.*

(d)   ♠ A Q J x x   ♡ x x   ◇ A K x   ♣ x x x

*With same auction as in example (b), this hand is too strong
for a 1♠ balancing bid. The proper bid is 2♠, showing a
good suit and 12-16 points.*

(e)   ♠ K x x   ♡ K Q x x   ◇ A J x   ♣ K x x

*After lefthand opponent has opened with 1♣, followed by
two passes, the proper call is double, since the hand is too
strong for a balancing bid of 1 NT.*

(f)   ♠ A Q x x   ♡ x x x   ◇ K Q x x   ♣ K x

*In the same auction as in example (e), a balancing double is
proper since the hand is too strong for a suit bid.*

(g)   ♠ x   ♡ A x x x x   ◇ x   ♣ A K Q x x x

After a 1 ◇ opening by lefthand opponent, followed by two passes, the balancer should cue-bid 2 ◇ since he would fear a penalty pass of a takeout double, and hopes to have the chance to show both of his suits.

ACTION BY THE PARTNER OF THE BALANCER

The partner of the player who balances must bear in mind that his partner does not promise as much strength in balancing as he would have done had he taken the same action in the immediate seat over the opening bid.

A game try is rarely called for unless the balancer's partner has at least 13 points. Balancer's partner will rarely have passed a hand worth 13 points unless he has a strong holding in opener's suit.

Even with 13 points, balancer's partner should be wary if the balancing action was a non-jump bid in a suit, showing 8-13 points.

With 13 points and a stopper in opener's suit, a player should raise to 2 NT if his partner has balanced with 1 NT. He should bid 1 NT if his partner has balanced with a non-jump bid in a suit. He should bid 3 NT if his partner has balanced with a jump bid in a new suit.

If his partner has made a balancing double, he may pass for penalties if he has K J 10 x or better in opener's suit, 13 or more points, and no other long suit. If he lacks the needed features to pass for penalties, the balancer's partner should jump in a new suit or in NT with 13 or more points. With less, he should make a non-jump response in a new suit, or in NT with a balanced hand and a stopper in opener's suit.

Alternative Systems and Conventions

WEAK NOTRUMP OPENINGS

Some partnerships agree that a 1 NT opening will show 12-14 high card points rather than the standard 16-18 high card points. The NT opener must have stoppers in three of the four suits and balanced distribution.

The chief advantage seen by the proponents of weak NTs is that a NT opening makes it difficult for the opponents to enter the bidding, and the frequency of the occurrence of hands in the 12-14 point range is nearly three times as great as that of hands in the 16-18 point range.

When the partnership has agreed to use weak NTs, if the opener instead opens in a suit and bids 1 NT at his second turn, he shows 15-17 points. If opener first bids a suit and rebids 2 NT, he promises 18-19 high card points.

Responses to the weak NT take into account the same distributional factors that influence responses to a 16-18 point NT. Opposite a weak NT, however, the responder needs a hand worth 12-13 points to try for game, 14-18 points to force to game, 19-20 points to try for a small slam, and 21-22 points to force to small slam. The Stayman and Gerber conventions are used with these point ranges in mind.

When weak NTs are being used, the opponents are more inclined to enter the bidding over 1 NT than they are over a strong 1 NT opening. Frequently, their intervention is by means of a balancing double by the player in the pass-out seat. To minimize the occurrence of being penalized in this way, if the partner of the NT opener has a very weak hand, he should respond to the NT opening rather than passing.

If he has a long suit in diamonds, hearts or spades he should bid it; without a long suit, he should bid 2♣ (Stayman), hoping to hear his partner bid a suit in which responder has three or four cards so that he can pass. Such an auction makes it more difficult for the opponents to enter, for responder could have as many as 11 points rather than none.

As a counter to this tactic, responder's lefthand opponent should normally double a 2♣ response whenever he holds 15 or more points.

FIVE-CARD MAJOR SUIT OPENINGS

Some partnerships agree that whenever one member opens the bidding with 1♡ or 1♠, he promises five or more cards in the suit opened. The principal advantage of such an agreement is that responder can raise opener's major suit with three-card support with much greater confidence. The raise has greater pre-emptive value than does a response of 1 NT.

Using five-card majors, opener will more frequently find it necessary to open the bidding with a three-card minor suit.

Examples:

    (a)   ♠ A x x x   ♡ K Q x x   ◊ x x   ♣ A x x

Opener would open 1♣.

    (b)   ♠ Q x x x   ♡ A Q x x   ◊ x x x   ♣ A K

Opener would open 1◊.

The agreement to open with a five-card major suit does not alter the standard rules as to the proper order in which to bid hands with 5-5, 6-5 or more uneven distributions. Thus, with a hand such as:

    ♠ A x x x x   ♡ x   ◊ A K x x x x   ♣ x

the bidding should still be opened with 1◊. The agreement is simply that if the bidding *is* opened with 1♡ or 1♠, opener will have at least five cards in his suit.

The principal implications of the five-card major style for responder are:

He should more often raise opener's major suit opening to the two level with only three-card support.

If the bidding is opened in a minor, he should normally respond in a four-card major suit if he has one.

He should be careful of raising opener's minor suit openings, for opener may well have only a three-card suit.

Examples:

    (a)   ♠ x x   ♡ x x x x   ◊ K Q x x x   ♣ x x

Opposite a 1◊ opening, this hand should respond 1♡. Opener may well have four hearts and three diamonds.

(b)   ♠ J x x   ♡ K x x x   ◊ K x x x   ♣ x x

Opposite a 1♣ opening, this hand should by-pass the diamond suit in order to bid its four-card heart suit.

(c)   ♠ A x x x   ♡ J x x x   ◊ Q x   ♣ x x x

Opposite a 1♣ or 1◊ opening, this hand should respond 1♡. The normal rule, that responder should bid the cheaper of his two four-card suits, applies when responder holds both major suits.

(d)   ♠ Q x x x x   ♡ A J x x   ◊ x   ♣ x x x

Opposite a 1♣ or 1◊ opening, this hand should respond 1♠.

(e)   ♠ A x x x   ♡ x x x   ◊ x   ♣ A K x x x

Opposite an opening bid of 1◊ or 1♡, this hand should respond 2♣, planning to rebid in spades. The fact that the partnership is using five-card majors should not lead responder to bid spades first, which would give a distorted picture of his distribution. A hand worth 10 or more points can afford to respond in a five-card minor suit before showing the four-card major.

FORCING 1 NOTRUMP RESPONSE

Most partnerships who use five-card majors also agree that a 1 NT response to an opening bid of 1♡ or 1♠ forces opener to bid once more.

Using the forcing 1 NT response, it is feasible to agree that a two-over-one response in a new suit is virtually a game-force. Thus responder could invite game in opener's major suit with 11-12 points by commencing with 1 NT and then raising opener's suit to the three level; this treatment allows the two-level response in a new suit to give the partnership the security of knowing that its subsequent bids are forcing until game is reached.

WEAK TWO-BIDS

The weak opening two-bid, used only in diamonds, hearts and spades (the opening 2♣ bid remains a strong forcing opening) is at once an offensive and defensive weapon. It is offensive because it promises a long suit with playing strength, and it is defensive because it raises the level at which the opponents may enter the auction.

The weak two-bid opening promises specifically a six-card suit, and a hand worth about 8-12 points with at least one defensive trick, but not more than two defensive tricks. The suit of the two-bid should be headed by at least the Q J 10. These requirements are frequently relaxed for a player whose partner has already passed.

Responder should bid game or force to game if he holds a hand worth 16 or more points. He should try for game if he holds a hand worth 13-15 points and a fit for opener's suit.

With fewer than 13 points, responder should raise opener's suit to the three level or four level when he has length in the suit and little defensive strength.

The response of 2 NT and any response in a new suit are forcing on the opener for one round, but neither response is forcing to game.

The 2 NT response does not normally suggest a desire to play the hand in NT, but rather asks opener to describe his hand further. The most commonly used method after a 2 NT response asks opener to:

Bid once again in a new suit with 11-12 points and the Ace or King (or, if necessary, the Queen) of that suit.

Bid 3 NT if his suit is headed by A K Q.

Bid three of his suit with a hand that is not appropriate for the other types of bids.

Examples:

(a)   ♠ A K x x x x   ♡ x x   ◇ x x   ♣ x x x

An average weak two spade opening. If the response is 2 NT, opener should rebid 3♠.

(b)   ♠ K Q 10 x x x   ♡ K Q x   ◇ x x   ♣ x x

Having opened 2♠, opener should rebid 3♡ with this hand to show a maximum, with high cards in hearts.

OGUST REBIDS

Some partnerships agree to give completely artificial meanings to opener's second bid over the 2 NT information-seeking response to the weak two-bid. These are called Ogust rebids and are designed to disclose whether opener has minimum or maximum strength, and whether his suit is robust or meager. The rebids are:

3♣	=	Weak hand, weak suit
3◇	=	Strong hand, weak suit
3♡	=	Weak hand, strong suit
3♠	=	Strong hand, strong suit

The determination of what is a "strong suit" in making and interpreting these rebids must always be done in the context that with any suit that is headed by the Ace, King, and Queen, opener will rebid 3 NT over 2 NT.

WEAK JUMP OVERCALLS

It has become increasingly common for partnerships to agree that a single-jump overcall directly over a one level bid shows a weak hand with a long suit.

The suit of the weak jump overcall should be at least six cards long and should be no weaker than Q J 10 x x x. The hand should contain fewer than 10 high card points and fewer than two defensive tricks. It should rarely contain a second suit; with a two-suited hand, a player should try to get to bid both suits to increase his chances of finding a fit with his partner.

Because the weak jump overcall is a pre-emptive bid made with few high cards, the Rule of Two and Three should be followed: if vulnerable, the overcaller should have playing strength that will produce enough tricks to ensure no more than a two-trick defeat; if non-vulnerable, he may have one trick less.

The weak jump overcall is not used over an opening bid above the one level. Over a weak two opening bid by an opponent, for example, a jump overcall shows an intermediate hand worth about 14-17 points with a good suit. There is no benefit in pre-empting over an opponent's pre-empt.

The partner of a weak jump overcaller normally has no reason to take optimistic action. The overcaller has shown few high card points and little defense, so unless the overcaller's partner has a very good hand, he should tend to pass or to raise pre-emptively; he needs a very strong hand to try for game or to double for penalties.

Examples:

(a)   ♠ x   ♡ Q J x x x x x   ◊ K x x   ♣ x x

This hand is worth a weak jump overcall of 2♡ over an opponent's 1♣ or 1◊ opening; but it is too weak for a 3♡ bid over 1♣, especially if vulnerable.

(b)   ♠ A Q x   ♡ K x   ◊ x x x   ♣ K Q x x x

Opposite a weak jump overcall of 2♡ over the opponent's 1♣ or 1◊ opening, this hand should pass.

FORCING STAYMAN

One variation of the Stayman convention is called Forcing Stayman. Like "non-forcing" Stayman, Forcing Stayman begins with a 2♣ response to a 1 NT opening, and asks opener to bid a four-card major if he has one.

The difference is that using Forcing Stayman, opener is not allowed to let the bidding die below the 2 NT level. (This variation does not, however, mean that responder cannot pass opener's first rebid.)

Example—If the auction started:

Opener	Responder
1 NT	2♣
2◊	2♡

Opener would be required to bid over responder's 2♡ call.

If opener has only a doubleton heart, he bids 2 NT; otherwise, he should raise hearts.

Using Forcing Stayman, the responder must have either a hand worth 8 or more points or a hand with a singleton club and length in the other three suits so that he can pass opener's second bid.

TWO-WAY STAYMAN

A very popular Stayman variation is called Two-Way Stayman. In its most prevalent version, a 2♣ response to 1 NT is used as non-forcing Stayman, and a 2◇ response to a 1 NT is used as game-forcing Stayman. Both the 2♣ and the 2◇ responses ask opener to bid a four-card major suit, if he has one.

The 2◇ response to 1 NT promises 10 or more points and commits the partnership immediately to game. If opener has a four-card major suit he bids it (bidding 2♡ if he has four hearts and four spades).

If he has no four-card major but has a five-card minor suit, he bids his minor at the three level; and if he has neither a four-card major nor a five-card minor, he bids 2 NT.

GAMBLING 3 NOTRUMP OPENING

Some partnerships agree to use a 3 NT opening bid to show a long solid minor suit with at most one stopper outside the long suit. The hope is that responder will have a few high cards that will enable the contract to be made. In any event, the high level of this opening makes it difficult for the opponents to enter the auction.

If responder's hand is very weak, or if 3 NT is doubled and responder lacks stoppers, he should bid 4♣ over 3 NT. This bid asks opener to pass if his suit is clubs or to bid 4◇ if his suit is diamonds.

If responder wants to reach game in a minor suit, he jumps to 5♣, asking opener to pass if his suit is clubs and to bid 5◇ if his suit is diamonds.

If responder has a self-sufficient major suit of at least six cards, he may bid it at the four level, requiring opener to pass.

A response of 4◇ over the 3 NT opening may be used to ask opener to bid his better major suit.

Examples:

(a) ♠ xxx ♡ Kx ◊ AKQJxxx ♣ x

Using gambling 3 NTs, this hand is a classic.

(b) ♠ QJx ♡ Qxxx ◊ x ♣ Kxxxx

Opposite a gambling 3 NT opening, this hand should pass. The smattering of values should be enough to make 3 NT a reasonable prospect.

(c) ♠ Axx ♡ Axx ◊ x ♣ KJxxxx

Opposite a gambling 3 NT opening, this hand too should pass. Game should be a virtual certainty, but slam is unlikely.

(d) ♠ xxxx ♡ xxxx ◊ xxx ♣ xx

Opposite a gambling 3 NT, this hand should bid 4♣.

UNUSUAL 2 NOTRUMP OVERCALL

The unusual NT overcall is a jump to 2 NT over an opening bid to show a two-suited hand. The bid normally shows at least 10 cards in the two lowest unbid suits. Thus, if the opening bid was in a major suit, the 2 NT bid shows the minor suits. If the opening bid was in a minor suit, the jump to 2 NT shows hearts and the unbid minor suit.

Bearing in mind that the 2 NT overcaller has about 6-10 high card points, his partner should take a preference between the two suits shown, and should do so at an appropriate level. He should pre-empt at the four or five level with a weak distributional hand

and with a fit for one or both of overcaller's suits; otherwise, he should show his preference at the three level.

Examples:

(a)   ♠ x   ♡ x   ◊ K Q 10 x x   ♣ Q J x x x x

Over an opponent's 1♡ or 1♠ opening, this hand would jump to 2 NT.

(b)   ♠ A J x   ♡ x x x x   ◊ x x   ♣ x x x x

Opposite a 2 NT overcall promising both minor suits, this hand should jump pre-emptively to 5♣.

Declarer Play

THREE GENERAL RULES ABOUT THE
LIKELY DISTRIBUTION OF A GIVEN SUIT

One can be quite a successful player without knowing the precise percentage of suit divisions if three general principles are remembered.

1. **If the opponents have an odd number of cards between them in a given suit, it is likely that those cards will divide as evenly as possible.** It is better than a 50-50 proposition that five outstanding cards will divide 3-2, or that seven cards will divide 4-3, or that nine cards will divide 5-4.

2. **If the opponents have an even number of cards between them in a given suit, it is unlikely that the cards will divide evenly.** It is substantially less than a 50-50 proposition that eight cards will divide 4-4, or that six will divide 3-3, or that four cards will divide 2-2. The only exception is that if there are only two cards outstanding, they are somewhat more likely to divide 1-1 than 2-0.

3. **Smaller numbers of cards tend to break more evenly than larger number of cards.** Thus, three cards break 2-1 more often than five cards will break 3-2. Five cards will break 3-2 more often than seven will break 4-3. Similarly, four cards will break 2-2 more often than six cards will break 3-3. Six cards will break 3-3 more often than eight will break 4-4.

PROBABILITY TABLE

The approximate probabilities as to how outstanding cards in a given suit will divide are as follows:

NUMBER OF CARDS OUTSTANDING	POSSIBLE DIVISIONS	APPROXIMATE LIKELIHOOD	NUMBER OF CARDS OUTSTANDING	POSSIBLE DIVISIONS	APPROXIMATE LIKELIHOOD
2	1-1	52%	6	4-2	48%
	2-0	48%		3-3	36%
				5-1	15%
				6-0	1%
3	2-1	78%			
	3-0	22%	7	4-3	62%
				5-2	31%
				6-1	7%
4	3-1	50%		7-0	1%
	2-2	40%			
	4-0	10%	8	5-3	47%
				4-4	33%
5	3-2	68%		6-2	17%
	4-1	28%		7-1	3%
	5-0	4%		8-0	16%

PRIORITIES ACCORDING TO THE ODDS

Some of the choices dictated by the likely distribution of a given suit are as follows.

Declarer should take a finesse (50%) rather than play for a suit to break 4-4, or 3-3, or 2-2. An exception is that when a suit consists of a total of nine cards between the two hands with the Queen missing, declarer should cash the Ace and King rather than take the finesse.

Declarer should play for one suit to break 4-3 or another to break 3-2, rather than finesse in a third suit.

Declarer should play for one suit to be divided 2-1 rather than for another suit to be divided 3-2.

Declarer should play for one suit to be divided 3-2 rather than for another suit to be divided 4-3.

Declarer should play for a suit in which six cards are outstanding to be divided no more unevenly than 4-2, rather than take a finesse.

SPECIFIC SUIT COMBINATIONS

Examples:

(a)   *West*   *East*
         K J 10   x x x

A low card should be led from the East hand. Unless South plays the Queen, the 10 should be played from West. Two tricks will be won whenever South has the Queen—50% of the time. (Playing to the King, however, will limit the winners to one trick regardless of which defender has the Queen).

(b)   *West*   *East*
         Q J x   x x x

East should lead twice toward the West hand; this will en-sure one trick whenever South has either the Ace or the King or both the Ace and the King (a 76% chance).

(c)   West   East
             KQx   Jxxx

East should lead twice toward the West hand. This will win three tricks whenever South has the Ace and no more than three cards in the suit.

(d)   West   East
             AKQxx   xx

If all five tricks are needed, the Ace, King, and Queen should be cashed; this will provide five tricks little more than one third of the time.

If only four tricks are needed and there are no other entries, declarer should play low from both hands on the first round of the suit. This play is called a "duck", and is done principally to preserve an entry while establishing a suit.

(e)   West   East
             AKxxx   xxx

Only four tricks are available; but in order to take them without entries in any side suits, either the first or the second round of this suit must be ducked.

(f)   West   East
             KQxxxxx   x (NO ENTRY)

A low card should be played away from the long suit in the hope that, if there is a 4-1 break, that one defender holds the singleton Ace. If there is a 4-1 break and no singleton Ace, three tricks will be lost in the suit; if there is a singleton Ace, the losses can be limited to two tricks if the first card played by West is a low one.

(g)   West   East
           A Q 10 x x   x x x

A low card should be led from the East hand and the 10 played from West. If North wins with the Jack, the East hand is re-entered to lead toward West's Ace and Queen.

(h)   West   East
           A Q 10 x x x   x x x

The proper play to try to take all six tricks, is to lead low from East and put in West's Queen. If North wins with the King, West's Ace is cashed next in hopes that the remaining cards are divided 1-1. If only five tricks are needed, a "safety play" is available: cash the Ace, then lead toward the Queen. Five tricks will be won about 5 out of 6 times.

(i)   West   East
           A Q x x   J x x x

A low card should be led from the East hand and West's Queen played. If the Queen wins the trick, the Ace is played next, hoping the King is now unguarded.

(j)   West   East
           A x x x   Q J x x

A low card should be led to the Ace, then a low card led back toward the Queen and Jack. This offers the best chance of winning three tricks in the suit.

(k)   West   East
           A x x x   Q x x x

A low card should be led to the Ace, then a low card back. If North plays low, East's Queen should be played unless declarer is sure that South has the King, in which case, a low card should be played, hoping that South's King is now unguarded.

(l)   West   East
          Q 10 x x   A x x

A low card should be led to the Ace, and a low card played back and the 10 inserted.

(m)   West   East
          A 10 x   Q x x

A low card should be led from the West hand to East's Queen. If this loses to the King, the next lead of the suit should be from East's hand, and West's 10 inserted. This line of play wins two tricks unless South has the King and North has the Jack.

(n)   West   East
          A K x x x   J 10 9

A card should be led from the East hand and a finesse taken immediately against the Queen.

(o)   West   East
          A K x x x   J x x

The proper play is to cash the Ace and King of the suit, hoping the Queen falls doubleton.

(p)   West   East
           A K x x   J x x

The proper play is to cash the Ace of the suit and then lead low toward the Jack. This play wins an extra trick when the Queen is in front of the Jack. Playing the Ace and King in hopes of dropping the Queen doubleton is a decidedly inferior play, if six cards are outstanding.

(q)   West   East
           K x x x   Q x x x

The proper play in hopes of making three tricks is to try to guess which defender has the Ace of the suit, and to lead the first round of the suit through that defender. Then play low from both hands on the second round of the suit. This play wins if the Ace is doubleton, and if declarer has guessed correctly which defender has the Ace.

(r)   West   East
           A J x x   K 9 x x

If four tricks are needed, the King should be cashed, and then a low card led to the Jack. If only three tricks are needed, cash the Ace and lead low from the West hand. If North follows low, play the 9. This play guards against either defender's holding Q 10 x x.

(s)   West   East
           A 10 x x x   K 9 x x

If five tricks are needed, a low card should be led from either hand. Assuming that the first defender follows, both high honors should be cashed. This play wins five tricks less than one half the time, since the outstanding cards are not likely to be divided 2-2.

If on the lead of the low card to the first trick of the suit, the first defender plays the Queen or the Jack, the trick should be won, and the suit led back and a finesse taken against the other defender. This is an application of the Rule of Restricted Choice, which, simply stated, is that if two cards of equal rank are outstanding and a defender has played one of them, he probably does not have the other one.

If declarer can afford to lose one trick in the suit, he should lead a low card from either hand, and if the first defender follows low, he should play the 10 or 9. If the first defender fails to follow suit, declarer should play the high honor. This play guards against either defender's holding Q J x x.

(t)	West	East
	K Q 9 x x	A 10 x x

The proper play is to cash the King or Queen of the suit first, in order to be able to finesse against either defender for the Jack, if his partner fails to follow suit to the first trick.

(u)	West	East
	K Q 9 x x	A x x x

The proper play is to cash the Ace of the suit, because if North is void, finesses can be taken against South's Jack and 10. However, if South is void, North's Jack and 10 cannot be finessed on any line of play.

SAFETY PLAYS

The safety play sacrifices a trick in order to guard against a bad break that might otherwise cost two tricks in the suit.

A safety play usually consists of either taking a somewhat deep finesse or of declining a finesse. Safety plays are most often taken in the trump suit, but can be made in any suit.

Examples have been given above in *(h)*, *(r)*, and *(s)*.

PLAYING TO A DEFENDER'S LEAD

The following are the proper plays if East is declarer and South has led a low card in the suit.

(a)   *West*   *East*
              Q x   A x x

Declarer should rise with the Queen on the lead from South. He will win the trick if South has led away from the King.

(b)   *West*   *East*
              Q x x   A x x

Now West has an extra card in the suit so that it is not essential to rise with the Queen. If South has the King, the Queen can be won later by leading from East toward the Queen. Playing low on the first trick allows for the possibility that North has the King and will play it even though the Queen has not been played. If it is essential to maintain control of the suit, or not to lose any tricks in the suit, the proper play is to rise with the Queen.

(c)   West   East
               Q 10   A x x

Declarer must guess whether South is leading from the King or from the Jack. If he has both or has neither, declarer's play will make no difference. If South is leading from the King, declarer must play the Queen. If South is leading from the Jack, declarer must play the 10.

In a suit contract the 10 is the better play, since many players forbear to lead from Kings against such contracts.

In a notrump contract, the better play is the Queen, since against notrump players usually decline to lead from a suit headed by the Jack.

(d)   West   East
               Q 10 x   A x x

The 10 is the proper play, since if South has led from both the King and the Jack, the 10 will win and South will be unable to lead this suit again without giving declarer a third trick.

(e)   West   East
               J x   A 10 x

The proper play to win two tricks in the suit on the lead by South is to play a low card from West. In this way, East either will win the 10 if North plays low, or will capture the Queen or King with his Ace, and still have both the Jack and the 10 left with which to force out the defenders' remaining honor.

(f)   West   East
             K x   J x x

On a lead from South against a notrump contract, declarer should play low from dummy. This ensures a trick in the suit regardless of the location of the Ace and the Queen. In a suit contract, or if only one trick can afford to be lost in a notrump contract, declarer must guess whether South has led from the Ace or the Queen. If from the Ace, he must rise with the King; if from the Queen, he should play low from the West hand.

(g)   West   East
             K J x   10 x

The proper play from West is low. If North plays the Ace, South's Queen becomes finessable. If declarer makes the mistake of playing the Jack from West at trick one and North plays the Ace, he can no longer finesse South, for the Queen will be played to cover East's 10.

(h)   West   East
             A x x   J 9 x

Declarer should play a low card from the West hand; assuming that North wins with the King or Queen and returns a low card, East should play the 9.

(i)   West   East
             A x   10 9 x x

When a low card of this suit is led by South against a NT contract, declarer should rise with the Ace. If South started with a five-card suit, the suit may well be blocked, since

North probably has a doubleton honor. This play will produce an extra trick for East's 10 9 is North unblocks or South overtakes the blocking honor.

THROW-IN PLAYS

There are many instances when it is advantageous for declarer to have one of the opponents lead a particular suit.

Examples:

(a)   West   East
         ◊ A Q   ◊ x x

If North can be forced to lead a diamond, declarer will make two tricks. If the declarer must lead the suit himself, he will make two tricks only half of the time—the half in which South holds the diamond King.

(b)   West   East
         ♣ Q x x   ♣ J x x

If declarer must lead clubs himself, he is unlikely to take any tricks in the suit. However, if either opponent leads clubs, declarer will get a club trick.

(c)   West   East
         ♡ A J x   ♡ K 10 x

Declarer can take three tricks if he knows which defender has the heart Queen, but if either defender leads the suit, declarer will not be put to the peril of a guess.

(d)   *West*   *East*
         ◇ A 10 x   ◇ K 9 x

In order to take three diamond tricks, declarer needs to have a defender lead the suit.

In order to effectuate a throw-in that forces the defenders to play a particular suit, declarer must strip them of their cards in other suits, so that it becomes impossible (or unprofitable) for them to lead any other suit. He may do this by cashing enough winners in other suits so that the defenders have no other cards left in the other suits. At a suit contract, the declarer may be able to ruff a suit enough times so that neither he nor the dummy has any cards left in the suit and could ruff any further leads of that suit.

Examples:

(e)

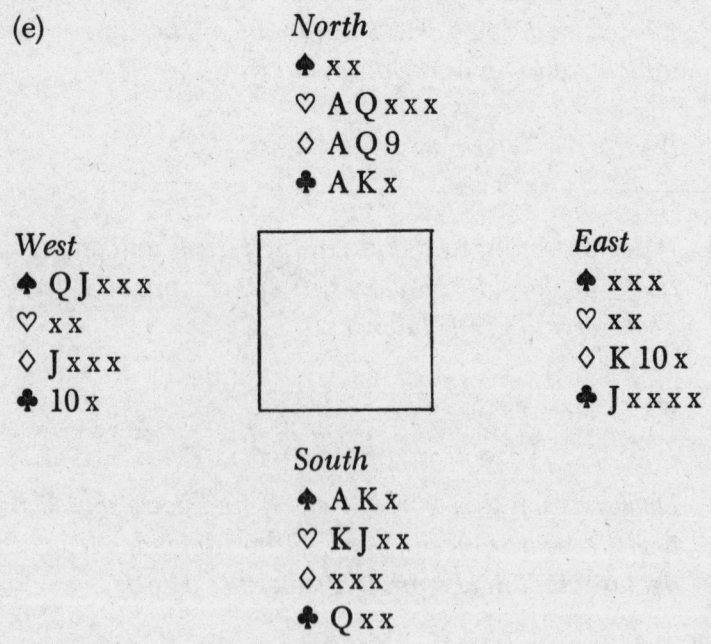

North
♠ x x
♡ A Q x x x
◇ A Q 9
♣ A K x

West
♠ Q J x x x
♡ x x
◇ J x x x
♣ 10 x

East
♠ x x x
♡ x x
◇ K 10 x
♣ J x x x x

South
♠ A K x
♡ K J x x
◇ x x x
♣ Q x x

South is declarer in 6♡ and receives the opening lead of the Queen of spades. He wins the King, pulls two rounds of trumps, then cashes the Ace of spades and ruffs a spade in dummy. Then he cashes three rounds of clubs ending in his hand. He leads a diamond toward dummy in this position:

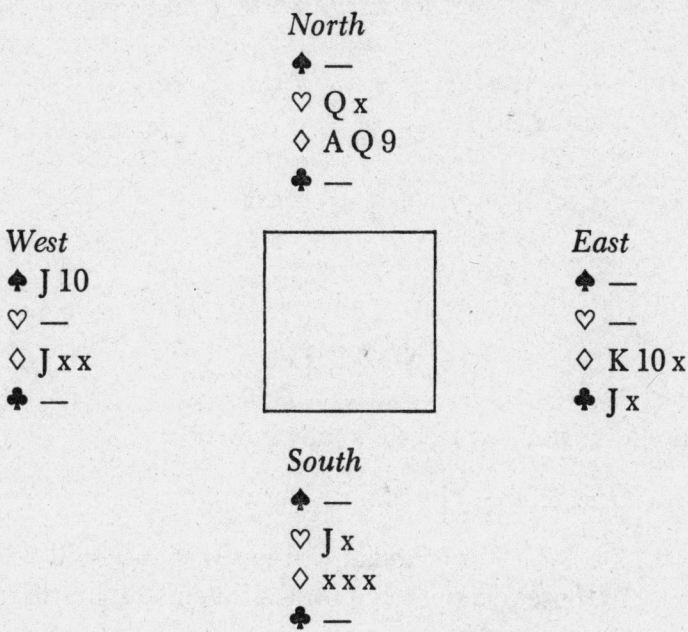

North
♠ —
♡ Q x
◇ A Q 9
♣ —

West
♠ J 10
♡ —
◇ J x x
♣ —

East
♠ —
♡ —
◇ K 10 x
♣ J x

South
♠ —
♡ J x
◇ x x x
♣ —

When a low diamond is led from South's hand, the defenders are helpless. If West plays low, North's 9 is played, and East, who wins with the 10, must either lead a diamond into the Ace-Queen, or lead a club, allowing South to ruff in one hand and discard the losing diamond from the other. If West plays the Jack, North's Queen is played and loses to East's King; but again East is forced to lead into a diamond tenace or to give a ruff-sluff.

Other combinations similar to the diamond suit in hand (e), in which declarer can lead a card toward an honor combination and gain a trick from the defender's return of that suit are:

(f)	West	East
	A J 10	x x x

(g)	West	East
	K 10 x	x x x

(h)	West	East
	Q J x	x x x

SQUEEZES

In its simplest form, a squeeze is a play in which:

(a) One defender has guards in two suits;

(b) Declarer has "threats," or cards that would be winners, in those two suits, but for the defender's guards; and

(c) Declarer has a winner in a third suit in which the defender with the guards is void.

When declarer cashes his winner in the third suit, the defender is "squeezed" out of one of his guards, giving declarer an extra trick.

For the operation of a squeeze, declarer requires the following conditions:

He should be able to win all but one of the remaining tricks.

He should have threat cards in two suits.

At least one of his threat cards should be accompanied by a winner in the suit.

At least one of the threats must be in the hand that plays after the defender who guards the two suits.

The defender with the guards should have no cards that he can afford to discard.

Examples:

(a)

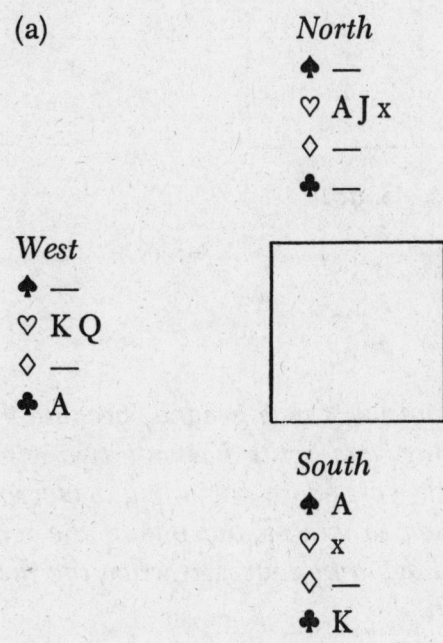

North
♠ —
♡ A J x
◊ —
♣ —

West
♠ —
♡ K Q
◊ —
♣ A

South
♠ A
♡ x
◊ —
♣ K

Declarer has three cards left, and has two winners, the Ace of spades and the Ace of hearts. West guards hearts and has the club winner, but has no more spades. When South leads the spade, West must discard either his club Ace or one of his hearts. If he discards the club Ace, South will cash the King of clubs and finally win the Ace of hearts. If West dis-

*cards a heart, South will lead a heart and take the last two
tricks in that suit.*

(b)

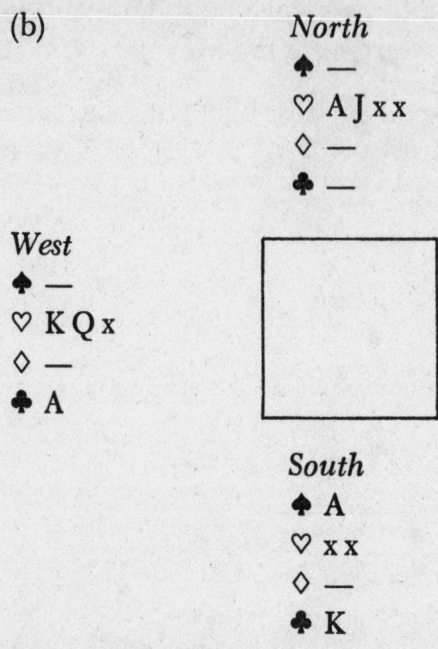

North
♠ —
♡ A J x x
◇ —
♣ —

West
♠ —
♡ K Q x
◇ —
♣ A

South
♠ A
♡ x x
◇ —
♣ K

*The squeeze does not work in this hand, because there are
four cards remaining, and South has only two winners. If
one of South's hearts were another winning spade, so that he
would be in position to win all but one of the remaining
tricks, West would again be squeezed when the three-card
ending was reached.*

If in example (a) East, rather than West, held the ♡ K Q and ♣
A, the squeeze would still operate, because the club King is in the
South hand. If the club threat were in the North hand along with
the heart threat, a squeeze could operate against West but not
against East.

Examples:

(c)

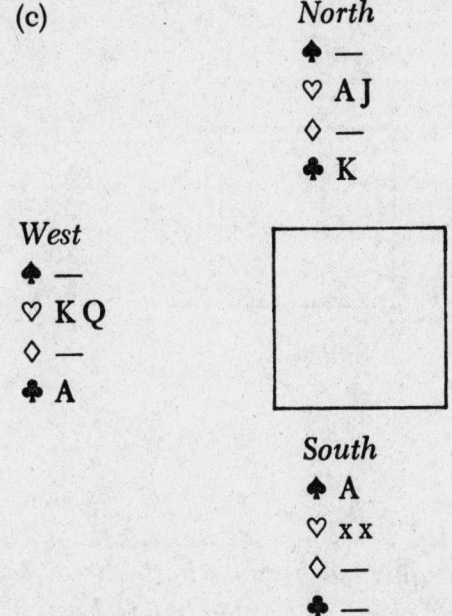

North
♠ —
♡ A J
♢ —
♣ K

West
♠ —
♡ K Q
♢ —
♣ A

South
♠ A
♡ x x
♢ —
♣ —

West is squeezed on the lead of the spade by South.

(d)

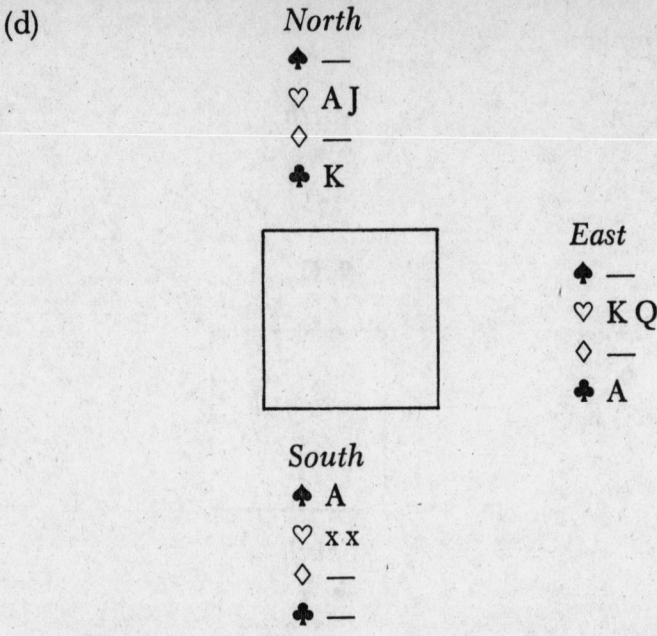

North
♠ —
♡ A J
♢ —
♣ K

East
♠ —
♡ K Q
♢ —
♣ A

South
♠ A
♡ x x
♢ —
♣ —

East cannot be squeezed because both threat cards are in North's hand and North must play before East. Thus, when South leads the spade, East will simply watch what North discards and discard the same suit.

COUNTERING THE DEFENDERS

There are certain plays available to declarer that do not necessarily relate directly to the establishment of tricks for the declaring side, but are rather steps taken to thwart the defenders in their attempts to defeat the contract. Among these are the hold-up, the avoidance play, and the loser-on-loser play.

THE HOLD-UP

The hold-up play is a refusal to win a trick in a suit led by an opponent. It is most commonly used in notrump contracts, and its usual goal is to break the opponents' line of communications in that suit.

Example:

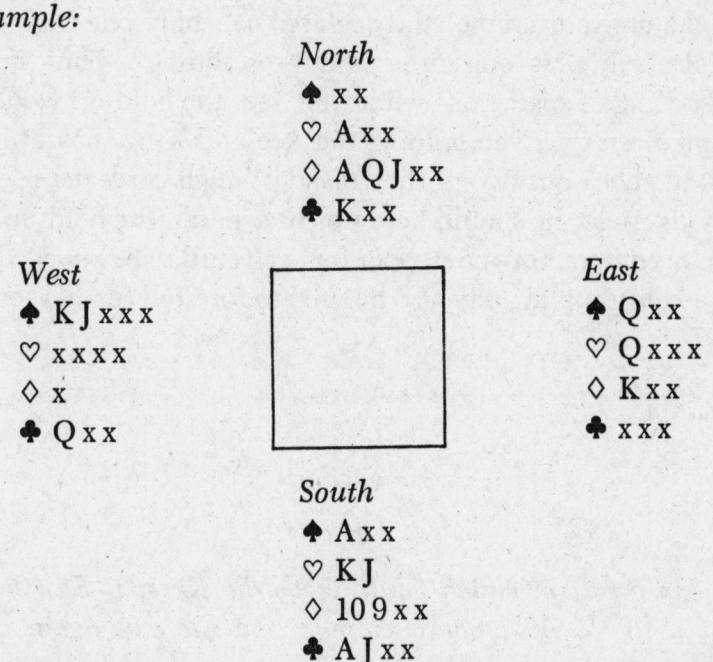

North
♠ x x
♡ A x x
◊ A Q J x x
♣ K x x

West
♠ K J x x x
♡ x x x x
◊ x
♣ Q x x

East
♠ Q x x
♡ Q x x x
◊ K x x
♣ x x x

South
♠ A x x
♡ K J
◊ 10 9 x x
♣ A J x x

South plays in 3 NT and receives the opening lead of the five of spades, on which East plays the Queen. South counts his winners and sees that if the diamond finesse wins he has 10 tricks, and that even if it loses he has 9.

However, when he counts his possible losers, he sees that he has cause to worry about the spade suit. If spades are 4-4 there is no problem since the opponents will be able to take only three spades and the King of diamonds if the finesse fails; but if the spades are 5-3, which is considerably more likely, they may be able to take four *spade tricks and the King of diamonds. Thus, South must hold up on the spade lead, and when East returns a spade at trick two, South should hold up again, in order to exhaust East's supply if the spades are 5-3 with East having three.*

In the above example, the declarer had only one high card to knock out before his long suit would be established. Thus, if he had held the King of spades as well as the Ace, the hold-up would have been unnecessary. Even holding the Ace and King, however, if he needed to knock out two of the defenders' high cards in order to establish his tricks, he should hold up. **In general, the hold-up should be employed to retain one stopper for each card to be knocked out.**

The hold-up play may also be used to forestall further leads of a suit.

Example:

West	East
x x x	A J x

In a suit in which South leads the King, if East holds up with his Ace, South cannot lead the suit again without giving East an extra trick. This particular hold-up is known as the "Bath Coup."

DUMMY REVERSAL

The dummy reversal is a method of playing in which several ruffs are taken by the hand that, at the outset, had the longer trumps rather than by the hand that held the shorter trumps. The hand that started out being shorter in trumps ends up longer, and is the hand that is used to draw the defenders' trumps.

Example:

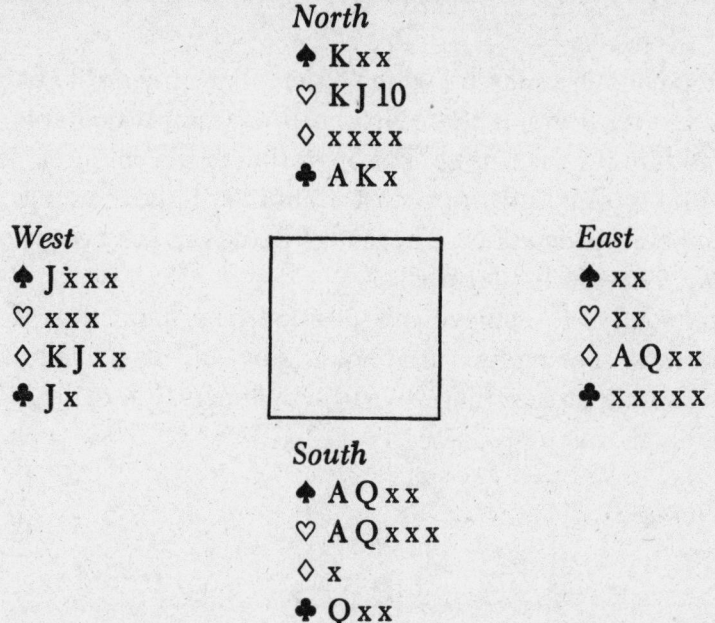

North
♠ K x x
♡ K J 10
◊ x x x x
♣ A K x

West
♠ J x x x
♡ x x x
◊ K J x x
♣ J x

East
♠ x x
♡ x x
◊ A Q x x
♣ x x x x x

South
♠ A Q x x
♡ A Q x x x
◊ x
♣ Q x x

South plays in 6♡ and receives a diamond lead and continuation. South has only 11 top winners—five hearts, three spades, and three clubs. The spades may provide a fourth trick if the outstanding cards break 3-3.

However, there is a better play for the contract: a simple 3-2 break in trumps (a 68% chance, as compared with the 36% chance of a 3-3 spade division) is all that is needed.

South ruffs the diamond continuation, leads a low heart to dummy and ruffs another diamond with the Queen of hearts. He leads another low trump to dummy and ruffs the last diamond with the Ace of hearts. He now leads a club to dummy's Ace, and pulls the last outstanding trump with dummy's 10, while he discards a spade. His slam is made thanks to a dummy reversal, with three heart tricks in dummy, three ruffs in his hand, three spades, and three clubs.

TRUMP COUP

A trump coup is a play by which a defender's finessable trumps are trapped, even though there are no low trumps available to lead through him for the finesse. For operation of the coup the declaring hand that is long in trumps must eventually have the same number of trumps as the defender. The lead of a side suit must come from the hand opposite the long trumps.

Frequently, to achieve this position, the hand that is long in trumps must shorten its trump holding by ruffing a side suit. When the shortening process involves ruffing winners, it is called a "Grand Coup."

Example:

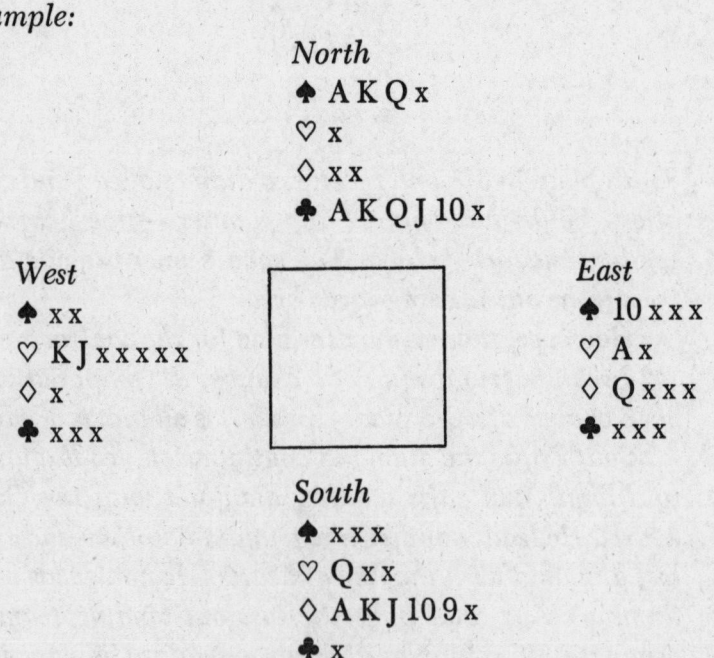

North
♠ A K Q x
♡ x
◇ x x
♣ A K Q J 10 x

West
♠ x x
♡ K J x x x x x
◇ x
♣ x x x

East
♠ 10 x x x
♡ A x
◇ Q x x x
♣ x x x

South
♠ x x x
♡ Q x x
◇ A K J 10 9 x
♣ x

South plays in 6◇ and West leads a heart to East's Ace. The heart return is ruffed in dummy. Declarer leads the remaining diamond from dummy and takes an immediate finesse in trumps. He then cashes the diamond Ace and re-

ceives the bad news that East started with four diamonds to the Queen. He must therefore ruff twice, to get down to East's trump length, and then contrive to have dummy lead on the twelfth trick.

Declarer leads a club to dummy and ruffs a good club, leads a spade to dummy and ruffs another good club. He leads another spade to dummy and now leads another good club, and East has no defense. This is the position:

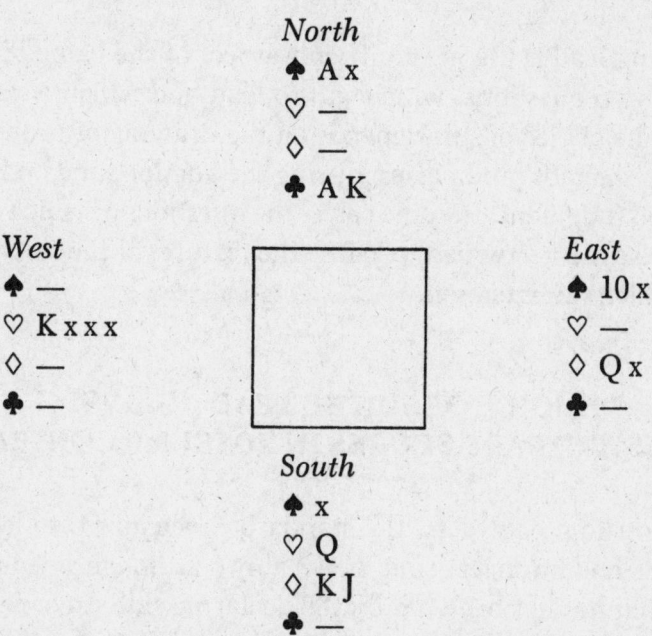

With North leading a club, if East ruffs, South will simply overruff and pull the last trump, discarding dummy's low spade, and use his last spade to re-enter dummy, which is high. If East declines to ruff, South will discard his losing heart and cash dummy's other high club, discarding his spade, then lead from dummy, couping East's Q x of diamonds with his K J. Note that if the Ace of spades is cashed in the above position before a club is led, East can defeat the slam.

Defensive Play

OPENING LEADS

The opening lead is the most difficult aspect of the game of bridge. There are two questions: which suit to lead and which card within the suit. The choice of suit depends on the drawing of proper inferences from the bids (and passes) during the auction, and on the exercise of good judgment. In some cases, the questions of which suit and which card are intertwined, because the textures of the suits may influence which suit is chosen.

CHOICE OF SUIT TO LEAD AGAINST
GAMES AND PART-SCORES IN NOTRUMP CONTRACTS

Against notrump contracts, the standard procedure is to lead from the longest and strongest suit, preferably—although not necessarily—one that has not been bid by the declaring side. In order of preference, the opening leader should lead as follows, *assuming his partner has not bid a suit:*

(1) Lead from a long, solid suit—for example, A K Q x, K Q J 10 x, or Q J 10 x x.

(2) Lead from a five-card suit—for example, A Q x x x.

(3) Lead from a strong four-card suit—for example, Q J 10 x, or J 10 9 x.

310

(4) Lead from a broken four-card suit headed by an honor or honors other than the Ace and Queen in combination.

(5) Lead from A K x in a suit not bid by declarer's side, hoping to hit partner with Q x x x x.

(6) Lead from four small cards.

(7) From a very weak hand, lead from a short suit trying to hit partner's long suit. The preferred lead is from two or three small cards in an unbid major suit.

If the partner of the opening leader has bid a suit, the opening leader should usually lead that suit unless he has a long solid suit of his own to lead.

If the opening bid was 2 NT or a standard 3 NT, make the safest possible lead. Lead from a sequence if possible. For example, a lead from J 10 9 is preferable to a lead from K J x x x against such a strong opening.

If the opening bid was a **gambling 3 NT,** lead an Ace; try to collect five tricks before declarer can run his long solid minor suit and whatever other winners he has.

CHOICE OF CARD TO LEAD AGAINST
GAMES AND PART-SCORES IN NOTRUMP CONTRACTS

If the suit to be led is headed by three cards in sequence, at least one of which is an honor, lead the top card.

Examples: *From K Q J x, lead the King.*
From 10 9 8 x, lead the 10.
From 9 8 7 6, lead low.

From a suit headed by two high cards in sequence, lead the top card if the third card is only one spot removed from the sequence; otherwise lead the fourth highest card.

Examples: From *K Q 10 x, lead the King.*
From *J 10 8 x, lead the Jack.*
From *K Q 9 x, lead the fourth highest.*

If the suit is headed by the Ace, or the King, or the Queen, and the next two cards are in a sequence headed by an honor, lead the top of that interior sequence.

Examples: From *A 10 9 8 x, lead the 10.*
From *K J 10 x, lead the Jack.*
From *Q 10 9 x, lead the 10.*

If the suit is less solid, lead the fourth highest card.

From four or more small cards, lead the fourth highest card.

From three cards headed by an honor, lead the lowest card.

From three small cards, lead the top card.

When leading a suit that has been bid by the opening leader's partner, it is proper to lead the top card from any doubleton, or from three small cards if the opening leader has raised the suit. But lead the lowest of three small cards if the suit has not been raised.

CHOICE OF SUIT TO LEAD AGAINST
GAMES AND PART-SCORES IN SUIT CONTRACTS

In leading against a suit contract, safety is a more important factor than length, since declarer will likely be able to ruff the defense's long cards. It is usually safe and desirable to lead a suit bid by partner.

If the partner of the opening leader has not bid, the best leads are from honor sequences.

The lead of an Ace is not usually advantageous. The lead away from an Ace is very rarely right.

The lead away from an unsupported King should be avoided.

The lead from a long suit is safer than the lead from a short suit, but is less likely to establish many winners for the defense. Thus, when choosing between Q x x and Q x x x x x, for example, if safety is the paramount consideration, the longer suit should be led. If the defense needs to establish tricks quickly, however, the shorter suit should be led.

When the opening leader has four or more cards in the trump suit, he should usually lead a long side suit. Such a long suit lead may force declarer to ruff enough times to promote the opening leader's trumps.

A side suit singleton may be an advantageous lead if the opening leader has trumps with which to ruff, and if he would not be ruffing with potentially natural trump tricks such as A Q or Q J x, or four trumps which could be promoted if he led a long side suit and forced declarer to ruff.

The lead of a side-suit doubleton is less advantageous, since it is less likely to produce ruffs. The lead of a small doubleton is most likely to work out well when the opening leader holds a quick entry in trumps, so that he may be able to interrupt the complete pulling of trumps, and can reach his partner to obtain a ruff.

Examples:

(a)   *West*
♠ A x x
♥ K x x x
♦ Q J 10 x
♣ x x

Against an auction of

South	North
1♠	3♠
4♠	

West should lead the Queen of diamonds, hoping to set up two diamond tricks to go with his high trump and his hoped-for heart trick.

(b)   West
    ♠ A x x
    ♡ K x x x
    ◊ x x x x x
    ♣ x

Against the same auction as in example (a), West should lead a club. Here, in contrast with (a), East may well have an entry with which to give West a club ruff.

Trump leads may be advantageous in some circumstances. However, a trump should not be led from vulnerable honor holdings such as Q x x. Nor should a trump normally be led from either a singleton or a four-card holding.

Trump leads are best when it is assumed declarer plans to cross-ruff the hand, or when dummy has exactly three trumps and holds a singleton or a doubleton, or when the defenders themselves have a great deal of high card strength.

A trump lead is mandatory when a takeout double on the one level has been passed for penalties by the opening leader's partner.

CHOICE OF CARD TO LEAD AGAINST
GAMES AND PART-SCORES IN SUIT CONTRACTS

From two or more honor cards in sequence, other than the Ace and King, lead the top of the sequence.

From the Ace and King (unless they are doubleton), lead the King.

From an interior sequence, lead the top of the interior sequence.
Example: From K 10 9 x, lead the 10.

From any other four-card or longer holding, lead the fourth highest.

From three cards headed by an honor, lead the third highest card.

From three small cards, lead the top card.

From a doubleton, lead the top card.

LEADING AGAINST A SMALL SLAM

Against small slams, the safest and usually best lead is from two top honors in sequence.

Lacking such a holding, if the bidding indicates that the declaring side has long suits that it can establish, an aggressive lead—a lead away from an unsupported honor—should be made.

If the declarer's and dummy's hands rate to be balanced, avoid leading away from unsupported honors.

The lead of an Ace should usually be avoided if it is in a suit bid by the declaring side, or if the opening leader has no other probable winners in his hand.

The lead of a singleton in a suit bid by the opponents should be avoided. The lead of a singleton in any suit should be avoided if the opening leader has a sure trick elsewhere. Otherwise, the lead of a singleton may be advantageous.

The lead of a trump against a small slam should be avoided.

LEADING AGAINST A GRAND SLAM

Against a grand slam, there is usually no need to be aggressive. If an immediate winner cannot be cashed, a safe lead should be selected. Frequently, a trump lead from a weak holding is appropriate, so long as partner is not likely to have a trump honor.

THE RULE OF ELEVEN

When the opening leader has led his fourth highest card in a suit, third hand can calculate how many high cards declarer has in that suit by using the "Rule of Eleven."

The Rule of Eleven states that if the size of the card led is subtracted from 11, the remainder is the total number of cards in dummy's, declarer's, and the leader's partner's hand that are higher than the card led. Thus, if the opening lead is the 7, third hand subtracts 7 from 11 and knows that there are only four cards higher than the card led in the other three hands.

Example:

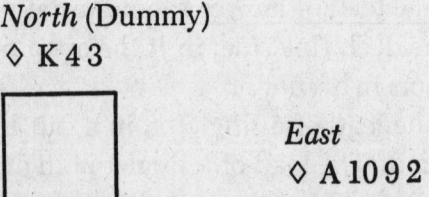

North (Dummy)
◊ K 4 3

East
◊ A 10 9 2

If the lead of the ◊ 7 is the opening leader's fourth highest diamond, declarer has no higher diamond. Thus, if a low diamond is played from dummy, East should play the 2, allowing West to hold the trick and lead through the King again.

PRESERVING COMMUNICATIONS

When the opening lead is from a short suit in which third hand has length and dummy has strength, third hand should duck to preserve communication with his partner. *Example:* If the opening lead against a NT contract is in a suit in which dummy holds K Q 10 and third hand holds A J 9 x x, when dummy's King or Queen is played, third hand should decline to play his Ace; instead, he should play the 9, an encouraging signal. Then when the opening leader gains the lead again, he can continue the suit to establish four tricks for the defense.

If the opening lead has been from a long suit in which third hand has the Ace and Queen, third hand should consider playing his Queen if the opening leader is unlikely to have a side entry to the suit after it is established by routine play.

Example:

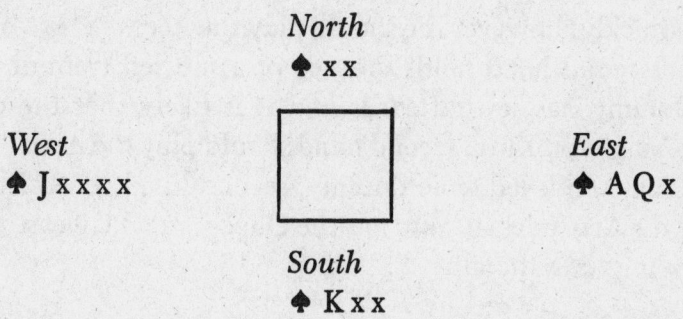

North
♠ x x

West
♠ J x x x x

East
♠ A Q x

South
♠ K x x

If, on West's opening lead of a low spade, East rises with the Ace and returns the Queen, South will hold up until the third round of the suit. If West has no side entry, the suit will produce no more tricks. If, however, East plays the Queen at trick one, South will usually find it irresistible to play his King at once, lest West have the Ace and South take

*no tricks at all in the suit. Once South's King has taken the
first trick, when East gains the lead he can cash the Ace and
reach West for the rest of the spade tricks.*

SECOND HAND PLAY

The term "second hand" refers to the first defender to play when a
suit is led by the declaring side. Either defender may be second
hand, depending on whether the suit is led from dummy or from declarer's hand.

As a general rule, when a card is led in a suit in which second
hand has non-touching honor cards, second hand should play low.

In general, when second hand has the Ace of a suit that is led toward several cards headed by honors in dummy, he should play low,
even though declarer may have a singleton. If second hand believes
that declarer does have a singleton and that the defense must take its
winners quickly, however, he should play the Ace.

When second hand holds the Ace of a suit led from dummy in
which dummy has several cards and it is likely that the declarer
holds the singleton King, second hand should play the Ace.

If a singleton is led from dummy, second hand generally should
not play the Ace unless he also has the Queen, in which case declarer
could not misguess the suit.

SIGNALING

There are essentially three kinds of signals that can be used by the
defenders:

(1) Signals that encourage or discourage the lead or continuation of
a suit.

(2) Signals that disclose how many cards the defender holds in the suit.

(3) Signals that ask partner to lead another specific suit.

"ATTITUDE" SIGNALS

In general, on an opening against a game or part-score, when a high card is led or one is played from dummy that third hand cannot top, third hand signals his partner to continue or to abandon the suit. When such "attitude" signals are given, a high card encourages continuation and a low card discourages continuation. For example, if the opening lead is the King of a suit in which third hand has Q 9 4 2, he would play the 9 to encourage his partner to continue leading the suit, assuming that he did not want his partner to shift suits. If he wanted his partner to shift suits, he would play the 2.

During the defense of the hand, attitude signals are generally given in suits led by the defenders, but not in suits led by declarer.

LENGTH SIGNALS

When the hand is being played in a slam, if third hand cannot beat the cards played to the first trick, he should give a length signal. Frequently, such a signal will tell the opening leader how to proceed with the hand. When length signals are given, the play of the lowest available card in the suit indicates that an odd number of cards is held; a high card, followed later by a lower card (called an "echo"), indicates that an even number of cards is held.

When the defenders follow to a suit led by the declaring side, whether from declarer's hand or dummy, the signals given, if any, are normally length signals rather than attitude signals. This is because a defender rarely wants to establish high cards in a suit that declarer has chosen to play. The defenders should not give length signals routinely, however, for declarer is free to observe them also. Such signals should be given only when the defender believes it will provide essential information to his partner.

TRUMP ECHO

When a defender wants to tell his partner that he has three cards in the trumps suit, the normal length signal is reversed. Thus, in trumps a high card followed by a low card indicates that three trumps are held.

This may be useful information if a defender is contemplating trying to give his partner a ruff.

SUIT PREFERENCE SIGNALS

Occasionally, a player may give a suit preference signal. This usually occurs when the opening leader wins the first trick, in a suit that third hand cannot want continued. In this circumstance, the play by third hand of an unnecessarily high card asks for the lead of the highest ranking other non-trump suit. The play of the lowest card held in the suit asks for the lead of the lowest other non-trump suit.